The Ecumenical Perspective and the Modernization of Jewish Religion

BROWN UNIVERSITY
BROWN JUDAIC STUDIES

Number 5

The Ecumenical Perspective and
the Modernization of Jewish Religion

by S. Daniel Breslauer

The Ecumenical Perspective and the Modernization of Jewish Religion

by
S. Daniel Breslauer

Scholars Press

Distributed by
SCHOLARS PRESS
P.O. Box 5207
Missoula, MT 59806

The Ecumenical Perspective and
the Modernization of Jewish Religion

by

S. Daniel Breslauer

Library of Congress Cataloging in Publication Data

Breslauer, S. Daniel.
The ecumenical perspective and the modernization of Jewish religion.

(Brown Judaic Studies; no. 5 ISSN 0147-927X)
Bibliography: p.
1. Judaism—United States. 2.Agus, Jacob Bernard, 1911- 3. Gordis, Robert, 1908- 4. Heschel, Abraham Joshua, 1907-1972. 5. Kaplan, Mordecai Menahem, 1881- I. Title. II. Series.
BM205.B73 296.3 78-9120
ISBN 0-89130-236-0

Printed in the United States of America
1 2 3 4 5
Edwards Brothers, Inc.
Ann Arbor, Michigan 48104

This study is the result of a year of research and discussion as participant in a seminar on Religion and Modernity: The American Case led by Professor John Wilson at Princeton University and sponsored by the National Endowment for the Humanities during 1976-77. The invaluable help of the seminar, Professor Wilson and the N.E.H. is gratefully acknowledged and appreciated.

TABLE OF CONTENTS

PREFACE

The idea of this book began when I noticed how similar a number of Jewish theologians sounded when writing about "biblical religion." Whether biblical scholars like Robert Gordis or philosophical commentators like Jacob Agus or poetic theologians like Abraham Heschel certain common themes resounded in their writings. My own training in the Hebrew Bible led me to be skeptical of theological exegesis while my grounding in the social sciences predisposed me to look to external forces to explain the trends I found. The more I investigated these theologies the more I became convinced that something broader than "biblical religion" or "Hebraic faith" was involved. These writers, it seemed to me, were united in an attempt to come to terms with American culture. Different as the various thinkers were their confrontation with modernity as expressed in American life brought them together.

During the academic year 1976-77 I pursued the clues I had discovered. I participated in a seminar sponsored by the National Endowment for the Humanities In-Residence Program held at Princeton University on "Religion and Modernity: The American Case." Under the guidance of Professor John Wilson the seminar explored the various models of "modernization" and their relevance as analytic tools for studying American religious life. In the course of the seminar a number of various concepts of modernization were discussed. The entire schema was often questioned as a whole. The interaction between scholars in such varied fields as American Puritanism, political science, sociology, comparative religious traditions, Judaic studies, and contemporary American history stimulated controversy while illuminating discussions by providing a variety of reflections on the same material. The complexity of modernization as a system of interrelated processes working in the political, ideological, social, and technological spheres encourages the multifaceted approach which the seminar developed. As the year of study progressed I grew to see that the Jewish case was best understood as an example of modern myth building. While social, political, educational, and technological issues were all important in the Jewish struggle with modernization even such a politically vital force as Zionism or the evidently pragmatic question of techniques of Jewish pedagogy could finally be reduced to the question of myth: how could modern symbols be evolved to designate and evoke the Jewish element in modern life?

My original plan had been to analyze four major theologians from the Conservative Movement in Judaism: Abraham Joshua Heschel--on whom I had written my Ph.D. dissertation at Brandeis University-- Robert Gordis, Jacob Agus, and Mordecai Kaplan--this latter was included even though he was an older colleague of the others because I thought I could detect in his writings a similar confrontation with modernity that I found in the others. I had expected to find each of them wrestling with the challenges of the modern political, social, cultural, and religious environment and restructuring Judaism accordingly. Using the normal categories of acculturation, assimilation, and cultural differentiation I expected to trace Judaism's attempt to meet the modern world and the accompanying religious compromises entailed.

Among the different Jewish religious groups in America it seemed to me that the Conservative Jewish movement took modernity most seriously theologically. Influenced by Marshall Sklare's classic study of that movement I saw it as a paradigm of American Jewry's attempt to maintain a balance between acculturation and survival, to meld into the modern scene but to remain distinctive. Sklare, however, had concentrated most of his efforts on delineating the folk religious culture. I hoped to use his same categories in a more detailed study of the religious elite or virtuosi whom he studied sociologically but not theologically. As I studied these theological elite, however, I found the normal categories of acculturation, assimilation, survival, and the like inappropriate. The elite response to modernity expressed itself less in programatic terms than in attitudinal ones, less as a proposal for ritual changes than as a mood of ritual awareness, less as a political platform than as an assumption about American political life. Whereas some observers had noted Conservative Judaism's lack of a consistent theology I found its elite representative of a rather pervasive "perspective," a way of looking at life that was recognizable and definable. This perspective can be understood as the most direct response which Conservative Jewish thinkers gave to the challenge of modernity.

This book is an account of the various facets of that perspective and describes its dimensions in the theological, ritualistic, political, and educational spheres. I call it "the ecumenical perspective" because its mythic vision sees all American religionists as housed under one roof, as sharing a single reality. Each segment of America's religious community is perceived as interrelated with every other, and the religious vitality of America as a nation is conceived of as dependent upon the cooperation of all groups. The theologians studied see their task as that of setting before American Jews the implications of Jewish religiousness not just for individuals but for the entire future of America. The theme of communal responsibility resounds in their writings. The weight of this responsibility bears most heavily upon contemporary Americans just because of the crisis of modernity. That crisis is interpreted as affecting all religiously sensitive persons. Jewish theological, ritual, educational, and political concerns are translated into symbols by which the common predicament of American religiousness can be understood. Judaism provides the language--or at least one of the languages--by which Americans express their religious discontent, their awareness of the spiritual malaise which afflicts contemporary man. Agus, Gordis, and Heschel help American Jews decode their tradition to unravel this message for modern man.

The ambiguous position of Mordecai Kaplan in the midst of these thinkers helps us separate an awareness of the modern situation on the one hand from the peculiar "ecumenical perspective" and its complex of ideas on the other. Kaplan does not seek to utilize Jewish symbols as metaphors for the American life experience--he tries to invent a powerful civil ritualism to fulfill that need. His theology *transvaluates* rather than *translates* Judaic concepts into the modern idiom. On one level Kaplan's cultural and social concerns renders him far more exclusivistic than those who share the ecumenical perspective. On the other hand his theology is a much more radical acceptance of modernity as an *accomplished fact* than it is a reflection upon modernity as a *predicament* or *situation*, the latter being far more expressive of the views of the other three thinkers. Yet despite these basic differences the common elements between Kaplan's assessment of the modern theological dilemma, the problematics of a modern Jewish ritual, the challenges facing Jewish education, and questions of Zionism and Jewish political thought and the assessment of the other thinkers is considerable. Studying Kaplan will at the very least help us point up the difference between seeing the problems and issues of modernity and offering an answer to them. More than that, however, one can find in Kaplan's exclusivism and cultural outlook a helpful counterpoint to the ecumenical perspective. The elite theology of Agus, Gordis, stands in sharp relief against the contrast of Kaplan's articulation of a folk religious tradition. One might even speculate that the popularity of the ecumenical perspective in contrast to the suspicion so often surrounding Kaplan's thought may have its roots in the "prophetic" distance separating its ideologues from the common practice and interpretation of Judaism.

Whether that speculation is justified or not, and without further empirical evidence about the comparative influence of these theories such justification is impossible, one would not be mistaken to see the power of the ecumenical perspective to lie in its mythological dimensions. Since the practical implications of the theories involved was less radical than the symbolism evoked, it is on that symbolism that we should focus attention. In this book the ecumenical perspective is taken as the blueprint of a new Jewish mythology, a mythology evolved in response to the problem of modernity. Theological writings and political musings are decoded in order to lay bare that animating myth which is hidden in the texts. In many ways such decoding is a common and familiar scholarly endeavor; it is the same type of detective work in which historians and sociologists are engaged. In the field of modernization, however, this approach is rather new. Even after Robert Bellah demonstrated that becoming modern involved changing from a traditional meaning system to a radically different moral and religious universe such changes were conceived in rather concrete terms--transformations of doctrine, secularization of rituals, abandonment of practices and the like. As the theologians in this book are decoded it becomes clear that modernization has a more subtle effect: the realignment of traditional religious elements so that they fit a new framework, a new mythology. While reviewing the theology, ritual, pedagogy, and politics advocated by these thinkers the underlying unity that weaves them into a new perspective on the universe emerges. Modernization involves a reevaluation of the entire world and environment of human life, of that world with which must reckon, the universe against which it must struggle.

Modernization, on this reading, can be described as a way of constructing the universe; in Robert Wuthnow's terms it is a "consciousness." Wuthnow's categories of theism individualism, social science, and personal consciousness are useful ones in a study such as this. They help locate the world-view of the ecumenical perspective in a geography of meaning systems. While one is tempted, like Wuthnow, to make this geography also a chronology--the social science and personal consciousness are "modern," the others are "traditional,"--it is more important to note that the theologians in question do not. Modernity represents the contest between these two world-pictures for them but is itself merely a condition, not a definition, of the world. The modern world is characterized by reference to these perceptual models--now it is explained by reference to social science, now by reference to personal consciousness. Its modernity, however, resides in the conflicts, the problematics that impinge on both social and personal reality. Religion becomes modern for these thinkers when it addresses the crisis which modernity has precipitated. Studying religious modernization is an exercise in the study of theological consciousness; decoding modern theology is an example of the ways scholars lay bare the implicit assumptions underlying explicit texts.

Both the realization that modernization is more subtle than usually realized and that the theological consciousness evolved a modern religious myth were cultivated through the seminar led by John Wilson. Without the opportunity to organize materials and ideas which the N.E.H. grant provided me I could never have had the leisure needed to penetrate the theological data. Without John

Wilson's broad knowledge of modernization literature and American religious history many central issues would have eluded me. Finally without the helpful criticism of colleagues I would have fallen into many more errors than now exist in the book.

Colleagues, both in specific comments and helpful remarks made in passing, opened my eyes to many gaps and inadequacies of my work. I hope the more obvious of these have been eliminated. Motivation to continue despite my knowledge that much has been left unsaid came from my hope that the book will prove useful to other students of religion seeking to decode and interpret man's varied religious expressions. My wife and family also deserve mention for the impatient urging they gave me, reminding me of the importance of this project. While I know that this book, thus, reflects the influence of many minds and the thoughts of many authors, I myself, naturally, take responsibility for all inaccuracies, infelicitous expressions, and errors that still remain.

I wish to thank *Forum* magazine for permission to use material that appeared there under the title "The Ecumenical Perspective and American Jewish Religion;" parts of chapter 5 appeared in *Conservative Judaism* XXI:1-2 (Fall-Winter 1976-1977) under the title "Modernization and Zionism in America," pp. 69-78; I thank them for permission to use those passages here.

CHAPTER I

THE ECUMENICAL PERSPECTIVE

Anyone reading Jewish history can hardly fail to notice the change in mood and attitude within the relationships between Jew and non-Jew that takes place in the modern period. While periods of toleration, productive intercultural interplay, and mutual respect between Jew and non-Jew can be isolated in the Jewish past, nowhere do we see the Jew embracing non-Jewish religions as partisans in a spiritual battle. Nowhere except in modern American Jewish thought do we find the affirmation that the Jew must stand beside the religious non-Jew in a confrontation with a demonic secularity. Naturally one can find within the Jewish tradition justification for such attitudes. The Jewish philosopher, Abraham Joshua Heschel, for example, had good Judaic precedent when he stated that "It seems to be the will of God that there would be more than one religion."[1] Upon investigation, however, the toleration and acceptance of other religious traditions Heschel advocated had its roots in a totally revised view of Judaism and the world. Heschel's ecumenical outreach was motivated by a sense of the desperate state of the human spiritual condition. He could agree with Jacob Agus that in such times different religions "can only regard each other as allies in the battle against nihilism and the quasi-religions of the day."[2] That this idea also motivated Heschel can be seen on further investigation. Heschel urged Jews to join with non-Jews because of the perilous state of the American soul. "Whether we like it or not," Heschel told his audiences, "the words we utter, the deeds we perform, affect the life of the total community."[3] While the "Jewish Mission" had been a bone of theological contention since the Enlightenment, this formulation of it was unusual. The Jew's task was to be deeply religious *Jewishly* and thus deepen the spiritual content of America *communally*. Just as the specifically Jewish treasure of the Bible became a world-wide influence, so it was felt a spiritually vital American Jewry would reawaken the religious life of all America. Robert Gordis suggested that for American Jewry to retreat to a religious isolationism, to ignore the implications of its religious life for the entire American community would be to betray "the spirit of the people that gave the Bible to mankind."[4]

These expressions of Jewish responsibility reflect a new way of presenting Judaism--a new self-presentation of the Jew. The background against which this new self-image arose was a political environment in which the American Jewish community struggled with issues of civil liberties and social justice for the entire American community, a religious setting in which dialogue and cooperation between religious leaders was stimulated and encouraged, and an intellectual community of universalistic thinkers.[5] This ecumenical context was the backdrop for the development of a new view of Judaism, a new theological stance developed by an intellectual elite. Practical activity and folk culture reflect the compromises made by men in their daily confrontation with concrete situations. The ideal self is often far removed from the realities of such folk solutions to daily problems. At the same time as these changes in practical activity are going on, however, there may be a change in the ideal. These two changes are not always completely synchronized; indeed if the ideal becomes too like the folk reality it may not be accepted by the masses. The ideal is rather the mythological creation of an artistic and intellectual elite. These elite leaders take the raw stuff of common experience, the perceived struggle between the ideal and the real, constructing from it a symbolic representation of that experience and struggle, transforming passing reality into eternal metaphor. In short the elite provide the folk with a myth, ritual, and self-consciousness. The theological affirmation of the Jew as partisan in a battle which musters all America's religious forces is an example of such a myth constructed by a modern elite.

Studying these thinkers is like studying any other religious tradition--one must discover the myths by which individuals interpret reality for themselves. In a modern context, however, the task is made more difficult. Unlike earlier myth-makers the modern theologian uses less explicit imagery, self-consciously avoids those mythic-pictures which would graphically reveal the model of reality he uses. Beyond the Judaic myth of the ecumenical perspective these thinkers have accepted a more basic myth--that of the modern world, certain expectations and assumptions about reality which already condition their self-presentation as Jews. After investigating the dimensions of this new Jewish myth--which we shall name the "ecumenical perspective"--we can turn to a discussion of modernization itself as a contemporary phenomenon.[6]

Diversity as a Positive Element

The new Jewish myth which we have called the "ecumenical perspective" is complex and composed of several elements. The simplest summary--that given above--suggests that it sees the Jew as part of a pluralistic religious setting. Taken at face value such coexistence might imply tolerance but not interaction, yet we have seen that this is not the case. The ecumenical perspective is founded on the assumption that diversity is creative, that pluralism is a situation in which various religious traditions interact with mutual self-respect and a sense of spiritual unity despite diversity. Jacob Agus describes the experience of pluralism as "the apprehension of unity and polarity, it is the awareness of a bond in unity in some sense along with the realization of categorical separateness and disunity."[7] The Jewish thinkers we are studying deny that a "common denominator" religiousness can be the basis of productive pluralism. Such a situation would reduce the power of each religious tradition and demand conformity rather than productive criticism. Men would become insensitive to the infinite variations of the ways in which it is possible to respond to the divine. This approach can be called "ecumenical" despite its affirmation of and even demand for separateness because it emphasizes that all these religious forms exist under one roof and strengthen the common house in which all live. Abraham Heschel makes this attitude clear when he states that "God's voice speaks in many languages, communicating itself in a diversity of intuitions. The word of God never comes to an end. No word is God's last word."[8] The implication here is straight-forward: if man wants to hear God's word he must listen to all the languages in which God has spoken. While God always addresses just this man in his unique language, God's message through this man is to all men. Diversity is productive just because it is a diversity within one household. Pluralism is creative just because it is ecumenical.

Heschel's defense of pluralism is clearly theological; other writers are more pragmatic. Jacob Agus suggests that the interaction of various religious traditions keeps them alive and responsive. Truly religious individuals, no matter what tradition they adhere to, should "welcome the challenge of differences in religion as the stimulus needed to keep the faith alive and fresh."[9] Here again diversity is creative in its own right. Differences in religious tradition are inherently good for *religion* as such. Variety is the means by which religions are prevented from stagnating, from being complacent, unimaginative, or locked into an unchanging routine. Such stimulating variety, however, is possible only when religions share a common universe of discourse, only when they inhabit a single cosmos. Once again religious pluralism is a force for religious growth only because it is also ecumenical.

The Depth-Dimension of Faith

The duality implicit in the concept of ecumenical pluralism is a stubborn problem. Where diversity is stressed as an inherent good, unity finds its grounding as an inescapable reality. Pluralism can be culturally cultivated; unity must be discovered as the underlying reality existentially as powerful for religious persons as is the diversity dividing them. Agus, Gordis, and Heschel found in what they called "the depth-dimension of faith" just such a unity. By this they meant the internal and personal experience of religion in contrast to its dogmatic and ritualistic expression. The external differences between one religion and another can easily be accounted for by reference to social and contextual elements; even a single religious tradition may admittedly evolve its credal and ritualistic system. The essence of religiousness, on the other hand, may be identified with the personal experience of meeting with God, a meeting that occurs in the realm of eternity not in the transient historical realm of social life. Abraham Heschel conceived of ritual and credal forms as opportunities presented to individuals, opportunities for stepping out of socially conditioned and historically limited time into moments shared with God. Since such moments share God's eternity they are free from the divisive and separating elements which differentiate one creed or one religious tradition from another. While rituals and dogmas separate men, Heschel claimed, the basic religious intuition is universal and unites them: "There are many creeds but only one universal faith. Creeds may change and develop and wither away, while the substance of faith remains the same in all ages."[10] The commonality of this faith joins adherents of various religious traditions into one community of faithful persons.

As a source of unity this faith needs to be made more specific and less undetermined; although basically a personal and private experience it cannot truly unite people unless it provides them with some common element of experience. Jacob Agus characterizes this element as man's soaring above the limitations of his historical and social boundaries. The religious experience is that of transcending conditions and limitations and expresses "a surge to the infinite horizons of man's spirit."[11] Such a faith is primarily critical--it rebels against chains and demarcations, against rigid and unbending structures. This critical thrust of faith helps explain its symbiosis with pluralism. Religion in its variety of guises is a spur to self-transcendence; it necessarily points beyond itself. The ultimate religious experience demands that the religious individual move beyond his closed circle, out of his narrow environment, and into a lived connection with others. Diversity is productive in this critical type of unity because by its nature it points to the insufficiency of any one answer; the unity which provides the commonality of all religious traditions is the recognition of that very insight! Pluralism is to be cultivated because the one ideal behind which all truly religious people are united, the one experience in virtue of which they can call themselves religious, is that of the need to expand boundaries! When Heschel informs us that "What all religions have in common is power to refute the fallacy of absolute expediency" he means to say that religions lift men out of a concern for the immediate, historical perspective to a higher, wider perspective.[12] The prophetic element in religion, at least as Heschel sees it, is not the concern for social justice as such but the demand for a view other than the conditioned, historical and socially limited one.

Models for Understanding the Ecumenical Perspective

The two basic elements of the ecumenical perspective from which all other implications flow are thus its affirmation of pluralism and its discovery of the depth-dimension of faith. How are these two fundamentals to be understood? Even the most superficial study of the Judaic tradition would reveal that this mythology is indeed a new one. It reworks older elements of the tradition, it is true, but its reading of Jewish sources is very selective, to say the least. The Jewish community has often been exclusivist, parochial, and hostile to outsiders. While the acceptance of other faiths that underlies the advocacy of diversity has its traditional analogues, the view of Jew as partner with the adherents of non-Jewish religions is totally unexpected. Similarly while the distinction between "duties of the heart" and "duties of the body" has a distinguished Jewish pedigree its use as a means of uniting Jew and non-Jew has little precedent. If the tradition is not the source of these ideas perhaps they can be explained by accommodation to the majority culture, acculturation to American life, assimilation into the general social environment. Such a facile model encounters the difficulties of the critical and self-affirmative aspects of the ecumenical perspective. Jewish religiousness is not to be compromised--only in its unique independence can it contribute to the creative diversity of American religious life. The general culture must be withstood, social convention is often to be resisted, technological life is to be opposed.

The popular model of assimilation is not complex enough to handle the transformation of Judaism represented by the ecumenical perspective. Jewish theologians were confronting more than an alien civilization; they were confronting a civilization in transition. Studies of modern society and more particularly of societies and nations undergoing the process of becoming modern deepen an awareness of the issues involved here. The crisis these thinkers addressed was not merely the contact of Judaism with another culture but the transition from a traditional social structure to a modern one. While models of assimilation and acculturation are not totally inappropriate in the study of the ecumenical perspective, models of modernization are more helpful.

There are a number of such models to choose from. Some emphasize economic facets of modernization, others stress political ones, still others psychological ones. While all models elucidate social transitions only one type of transition corresponds to that envisioned by the ecumenical perspective. It is necessary to find a model of the right type of transition. We can now examine the variety of models generated by modernization studies and decide which is most useful in this study.

One cannot deny that the ecumenical perspective has political implications. Not only Zionism which is the most unabashedly political expression of this theology, but the entire complex of ideas associated with depth-theology resound with political meaning. The ecumenical perspective calls upon Jews to stimulate a sensitive religious approach to political issues. Agus, Gordis, and Heschel were active leaders in the movement for civil rights, pacifism, and economic reforms. They supported their involvement by stressing the practical consequences of the depth-dimension of faith. Because faith provides a criterion other than expediency by which to judge human action it also provides a critical opposition to a self-interested politics. The religious vision is seen as a powerful political force which challenges the crass assumptions of professional politicians.

Various studies conducted in modernizing countries suggest that religions often play such an adversary role in modern politics. One of the essential features of political modernization is the broadening of the political base. More and more members of a society become active in political life and the government is expected to be more responsive to a greater number of constituents. In such a situation the basic issue is that of legitimating both individualism on the one hand and political order on the other. Political religion arises as a symbolic expression of discontent--either because expectations for civil liberties have been unfulfilled or because an intense individualism has corroded the sense of social unity upon which a nation depends. One group of models to which we might turn see this issue of political religion as most crucial. Religious change in modernizing nations is understood as part of the process by which a national group grapples with the problem of individualism and unity.

David E. Apter describes such political religion as a means by which man's sense of the human community is given a sacred authority. Social ideals become sacred ideals and are invested with ultimate significance. "Political religion," he suggests, "fits individual moral purposes and life chances to technological dynamism. Individual roles are acceptable only in so far as they enlarge that dynamism and share in it."[13] In this way political religion overcomes both the lack of social cohesion and the temptation to totalitarianism to which modernization could lead. Still Apter is uncomfortable with political religion and sees it as dangerous. Others, however, claim that political religion, because it utilizes traditional symbolism, can provide the best impetus to modernization a society can have. Political religion, according to this approach, enables traditional elements in society to become participants in political life far more readily than they would have otherwise: "The effort to define a national heritage in the form of a set of continuing traditions is also a way of coping with the wide gap that separates elite and mass, city and village, region and region . . ."[14] Seen from this perspective political religion is an intrinsic element in modern government. Its rituals and symbols provide the cement that unites a disparate nation. Ideologically it affirms individualism while structurally binding the community into a totality.

Certainly Agus, Gordis and Heschel display a concern and high regard for individuals together with the sense of total community characteristic of political religion. The ecumenical perspective demonstrates a profound political sensitivity and addresses the political problems of modernity. It enriches our understanding of this theology to see its contribution to American political life. Yet can we call this theology political religion? Does this model help explain the ritualistic changes and theological innovations of the ecumenical perspective? I think not. There are too many loose ends that cannot be tied together. Theological musings unrelated to political issues characterize much of the writings we will study. Ritual was certainly often conceived of as relevant to society but it was not directly linked to political programs. While the meaning of Jewish symbols was offered as a model of modern religious sensitivity, these thinkers did not suggest that all Americans accept the symbols and myths derived from Judaism. Even the Bible which, as we shall see, was seen as central to ecumenical theology, was interpreted as a compendium of mixed symbols and myths whose importance lay in its very ambiguity. Political elements in religion were not ignored but Jews stressed a more universal conception of religion in general and a greater diversity of symbolism than is present in political religion. While the model of political religion illuminates some underlying consequences of the ecumenical perspective it is too limited to be the basic concept through which that perspective is investigated.

A second approach would be to see the ecumenical perspective as a means of coping with the changed self-image arising from modern society. Some thinkers explain religion as a means of supplying "the world with a structure of symbolism which will articulate, not explain, the mysteries of human existence and give man some inkling of ultimate purpose in life."[15] The modern world, however, is a world of techniques and religion seems irrelevant to men "thoroughly habituated to expect that there is a technique to meet every need."[16] If religion is to survive in this type of a milieu it must become "compatible with high levels of modernization."[17] One of the consequences of this change is that religion becomes focused on the individual and his needs. It too is conceived of as a technique--a technique for coping with life. This individualistic model of religion sees it as providing for self-expression and ministering to the needs of the person. A sign of such modernization (others call it "secularization" or "atomization") of the religious purpose is that "religious groups cease to interpret the world in terms of external control and begin to interpret it in terms of internal participation."[18] The distinction involved here is that between religion as an imposed structure historically given and that of personal, individual religiousness as a means of making sense of the world. A look at the psychological interpretation of religion given by such thinkers as Gordon Allport and Abraham H. Maslow reveals similar views. "If organized religion has any ultimate effects at all," Maslow claims, "it is through its power to shake the individual in his deepest insides."[19] Society, this view suggests, is merely the context for individual self-exploration. Religion needs to adjust itself to this situation and become a tool for the individual. Gordon Allport criticizes social scientists who fail to see that the essential element in religion is the participant. Social cohesion may be a result of religious belief, but Allport suggests it cannot be its motivation. "The person who conforms to a religious custom," Allport argues against sociologists, "does so for his own private reasons and derives from his conformity some special significance for his own life."[20] Traditional religions are expected to transform themselves so that this individualism becomes more manifest in their self-presentations.

This model of transition from social entity to privatized tool for personal self-development helps explain the intense individualism present in the ecumenical perspective. Not merely is there a lack of institutional competition but even within an institution variety and diversity is cultivated. The emphasis placed upon the depth-dimension of faith is a clear recognition that the individual is central to religion. None of the thinkers we shall study deny Judaism's traditional concern for the community. All of them, however, contend that the individual is primary. By remolding Jewish life to fit the ecumenical perspective these theologians also made it more individualistic and privatized. The interpretation of Zion as a depth-dimensional concern for persons or of the Sabbath as a personal experience of transcendence is more than a means of coping with social pluralism. It is also a way of presenting Judaism as personally relevant, as a technique for individual self-fulfillment. The model of the transformation from social religion to psychological religion illuminates the references to insight, inspiration, and self-exploration that abound in the writings of Agus, Gordis, and Heschel. God becomes a symbol not of the social system but of man's striving for personal perfection; ritual provides an opportunity for self-transcendence not for social solidarity; political symbols project an inner reality, not an external concern for expediency.

Given this psychological concern, how was it possible to avoid a social isolationism? Would not such a concern for self stimulate a withdrawal into the private realm of personal reality? Such an abandonment of social responsibility did not actually occur. Agus, Gordis as well as Heschel are careful to affirm the need for Jews to act for the social good. While the model of a transition to psychological religion helps explain much of what lies behind the ecumenical perspective it fails to account for the social conscience associated with that perspective. To use this model would be misleading for it would focus on only one element in the development of that perspective. It could not analyze the necessity to grapple with political imagery rather than to avoid it completely.

A related approach would see religious rituals as private dramas expressing public realities. Modernity would imply not technological society but the variety of social relationships and public roles individuals play. Religion, using this model, has the task of teaching in symbolic language the variety of public personas available to modern mad. It is possible to use old symbols to express new relationships and thus overcome the trauma of social change. In modern society, it has been suggested, traditional symbols play just this role. Symbolism provides a sense of continuity even while tremendous alterations of social reality are being achieved. The basic premise of this model is that "Symbols are objects, acts, relationships or linguistic formations that stand *ambiguously* for a multiplicity of meanings, evoke emotions, and impel men to action."[21] Symbols are codes for social meanings. They act as a training in correct and incorrect action. Rituals "function as names which signify proper, dubious, or improper ways of expressing relationships."[22] To modernize ritual means to choose that meaning which corresponds with the modern social setting.

The model underlying this view of religion would be that of determining one set of meanings rather than another as representative of a symbolic system. The ways in which theology, ritual, or political symbolism are changed would reflect realistic assessments of the social situation. Symbols are seen as multi-dimensional; transition involves selecting one out of a number of meanings possible for a specific symbol. Change can be studied by looking at the social reality symbols are meant to express. As private dramas, rituals must be effective in impelling individuals to action. They must grow out of the individual's condition and correspond to his internal reality. At the same time their ultimate goal is social and their basic meaning derives from the social structure. Here we find a combination of the social determinism found in the political model and the psychological focus of the individualistic model. Both personal meaning and transpersonal cultural conditions are relevant to a study of religious change, according to this approach.

The duality revealed by the model of religious change

as reflecting social relationships is one strong argument in its favor. The complexity of the ecumenical perspective demands that we use a complex model to understand it. One cannot help but feel, however, that both the personal reality to which this model points and the social structures it posits are irrelevant to the theologians under discussion. They are not seeking to provide modern man with a personal vocabulary which can translate social realities into mythic dimensions. Their awareness of society is bounded by institutions rather than interpersonal relationships. Their concern with the self is inner-directed rather than oriented to external life. The social image they project is an idealized one. The relationships they inculcate between religions or nations are not yet achieved; they offer symbols for goals to be sought rather than actualities already in existence. Their image of the self perceives the individual as a world of his own, as a locus for private experience. While the individual grows through responsible interaction with others this interaction occurs spontaneously rather than through formal patterns of communication. While the model of religion as a code pointing to social relationships helps us see the complexity of the ecumenical perpsective it misses the self-definition these thinkers had. Of course it can be argued that behind their self-definition lay an actual use of religion as a social metaphor. This model is useful by drawing attention to that possibility. To begin with the model as an actual fact, however, rather than as a mere possibility would be to bias the data and would obscure some facets of the ecumenical perspective that might be intrinsic to our understanding of it.

There is a final model that we might use--that of "consciousness." Consciousness can best be described as a sense of that framework within which we experience reality. Consciousness refers to the way in which the separate events of life are woven together to form a unified whole. "Human consciousness," Robert Wuthnow informs us, "as the process by which reality is constructed, needs to be recognized as not simply a psychological phenomenon, but as a process linked in important ways to the functioning of society."[23] Consciousness is more than either a symbolic representation of social relationships or a personal vision of reality. It includes both of these facets as the basic structure which binds personal existence and social behavior into a holistic pattern. Consciousness is more than a reflection of society or personality, it is the criterion by which we decide what is *real* in society or self and what is illusory.

The model we can construct based upon the idea of consciousness can incorporate and go beyond those previously advanced. This model suggests that changes in religion are attempts to bring religious claims within the boundaries of perceived reality. As the perception of reality changes so, it would be expected, the perception of religious claims would also change. Robert Wuthnow's study of the San Francisco Bay Area supports the thesis that Americans have an altered consciousness. Whereas earlier generations saw reality either as a function of individual self-expression or as the result of a creative divine act, modern people seem to focus on reality as either the product of impersonal social forces or as a personal, inward vision. As with the earlier views so with the modern ones there is often a mixed consciousness--some reality is perceived as belonging to one sphere and some to another. The modern man often divides his world into social realities and inner realities.[24] One might posit that religious thinkers would seek to convert their claims into one or another of these categories.

The usefulness of this model for our purposes is that it will facilitate the study of seeming contradictions. The mixture of social awareness and inner-directedness which characterizes the ecumenical perspective can be illumined by Wuthnow's model. Since that model is a complex one the variations between theologians who share the ecumenical perspective can be accommodated. Using the model of a changing consciousness permits us to be responsive to both the pluralism and the affirmation of unity found within the ecumenical perspective. Wuthnow suggests that the social consciousness sees the world as a series of pressures and stimulii which condition human actions. Social determinism creates a world in which men respond according to the variety of influences pressing upon them. The stress on pluralism found within the ecumenical perspective can be interpreted as a tool by which this social consciousness is integrated into Jewish religion. The necessity of contextually determined differences, the inevitable distinctions between one person and another, between one community and its neighbor, are all subsumed under this social consciousness. Using Wuthnow's model we can see pluralism as the means by which the ecumenical perspective modernizes Jewish religion--that is makes its meaning system intelligible given the world as constructed by social science.

At the same time that individuals accept the social consciousness they may also reserve a space of reality free of such determinism. His findings show that there is no inherent contradiction in holding both the social scientific and the "mystical" (or personalist) consciousness. The ecumenical perspective makes room for this construction of reality as well. The emphasis upon depth-faith affirms the personal reality of transcendent meaning. This reality is free from the determinism of the external world and can therefore promise a greater unity and universality than the social consciousness. Depth-dimension faith is a means by which theologians can translate their religious tradition into the reality established by the personal consciousness.

Using Wuthnow's model we find the process of modernization exemplified by the ecumenical perspective to be that of translating from one symbolic idiom to another. The idiom of religious language is translated into either the idiom of social scientific consciousness or the idiom of personal (mystical) consciousness. To become modern means neither to acculturate or assimilate into a majority culture but to rephrase the traditional metaphors of a religious heritage into a style congruent with the world-view of its adherents. The study of the ecumenical perspective, then, is an investigation of how theological language, ritual behavior, educational theory, and political concerns are rendered in terms of worlds conceived of either under the aspect of social science or personal consciousness.

At this point is is impossible not to mention the theological writings of Mordecai Kaplan. More than any other American Jewish thinker Kaplan set out on the task of translating traditional Judaism into contemporary terms. Kaplan self-consciously sought to remold Jewish thinking about God, ritual, education, and politics into the framework of democratic American reality. If anyone in American Jewish life could be said to be a modernizer it must be Kaplan. Can he be considered a representative of the ecumenical perspective? I, for one, certainly thought so at one time. I no longer do so, for reasons that I hope to make clear at the end of this book. Kaplan's model of modernity is far different than those sharing the ecumenical perspective and as a contrast to them his writings are particularly illuminating. The ways in which they struggled with the meaning of a modern Judaism can be seen as more distinctive when placed along side of Kaplan's. His theology, views on ritual, and approach to Zionism recall alternative models of modernization and can correct the impression that the "consciousness" model is the exclusively adequate one. Its adequacy for the ecumenical perspective remains to be shown, its adequacy as a comprehensive and total explanation of Jewish attempts at modernization is not even being suggested. While this study focuses on the mythology derived from the ecumenical perspective it should not be forgotten that American Judaism is best described as a cluster of competing mythologies rather than as a normative mythological system.

CHAPTER II

BELIEF IN THE GOD OF ISRAEL

The Evolution of a New View of God

The study of Jewish philosophy is the study of a succession of philosophical systems. As one influence after another permeated the Jewish world, Platonic, Aristotelean, Kantian, and Hegelian theologies developed in response to perceived philosophical realities. The study of Jewish thought is very often a search for philosophical pedigrees, for the roots of a particular Jewish theological system in both the Jewish past and in the culture from which it derives. Such a philosophical analysis is useful and interesting, but it can be augmented by a social and psychological probing into the function of theology. While some theoreticians maintain that religion has a "functional definition" others would contend that religion has different functions in different social settings. This study assumes the latter position. Our first question, then, will be what function does the belief in God have for Jews sharing the ecumenical perspective? Does the idea of God interpenetrate the affirmation of a pluralistic social structure and the individual's private, inner reality which characterizes the modern consciousness? Does the belief in God motivate inner exploration or heightened social consciousness? If it does not, how do these theologians reconcile theology with their view of the world?

Belief in God has served, traditionally, to legitimate the Jewish legal system and to justify the survival of the Jew as a unique social being, as a member of a specific national and cultural group. The law which marks the Jew as different from others and the sense of distinction through a holy task have both been grounded in the Jew's belief in an all-powerful deity who chose the Jew and gave him the law. Beyond these explicit functions belief in God, according to certain psychologists, has offered the Jew a model of human potential and elevated his personal strivings to a metaphysical level. Belief in God, accordingly provides a role model which exalts the human being and engenders a set of personal expectations and obligations which are internalized. Erich Fromm, for example, assumes that belief in God plays just this role when he argues that God must be "a symbol of *man's own powers* which he tries to realize in his life, and is not a symbol of force and domination, having *power over man*."[25] Gordon Allport conceives of mature religion as utilizing belief in God to support the individual's dynamic potential and as providing "motive power to live in accordance with an adequate frame of value and meaning;" such a view, he claims, will be able to "enlarge and energize this frame."[26] Authoritarian religion, in contrast to a humanistic religious belief in God, is seen as repressing self-expression. Psychologists characterize belief in God as immature when "rather than admit criticism . . . (it) fights intolerantly all attempts to broaden it."[27]

Another aspect of the psychological interpretation of belief in God focuses on "the inner experience not of need but of fulfillment," which some claim is "the inner dimension of transcendent reality."[28] It is worth asking how belief in God can accomplish this. The idea of God as role model is the primary element involved. Not only is God's transcendence the basis upon which the individual intuits his own ability to experience fulfillment, but God's own ambivalence is a model of man's. Monotheism, it can be argued, enables man to uncover both the darker and lighter aspects of his personality because the idea of one God implies that both good and evil are contained in the Godhead.[29] God in monotheism is, at least subconsciously, a God in conflict with himself. Whether tradition admits it or not, psychologists find that in the Judeo-Christian tradition, "The Godhead itself is also imperfect because, and in so far as, it contains within itself the principle of opposites."[30] This approach to the function of belief is an important element in the modern interpretation of

Judaism. While the "oceanic feeling" of unity with all creation was traced by Freud to infantile emotions, modern theologians can call upon respected psychological opinion to support their religious claims. They can advance belief in God as an aid to personal growth and development, they can point to God as a role model for the struggle against inner weakness and the resolution of internal conflicts. Even the "oceanic feeling" can be put to good use as a motive for personal and social cohesion. The mature religionist, one psychologist suggests, holds a belief in God that will stimulate "the experience of oneness with the All, based on one's relatedness to the world as it is grasped with thought and love."[31] Believing in God means affirming the transcending unity which binds diverse peoples into a whole humanity.

Finally the social importance of belief in God should be mentioned. Sure belief is, if not the cause then, an expression of a coherent worldview. God becomes, on this account, a metaphor for the meaning and purposefulness of the world. Belief in God is, as it were, a code, a condensed expression of a set of practical propositions about living. As a construction of the world belief in God can be conceived of as an insight which "confers intelligibility and direction upon conduct."[32]

The foregoing sketch does not attempt to summarize the major trends in the psychology of belief or even hint at the variations among theories in psychology and sociology concerned with believing in God, with theology, theodicy, or related issues. Modern psychological and sociological theory has, however, shifted the perspective on the function of belief. The traditional issues of legitimation of Jewish survival and Jewish law have now been augmented with the questions of God as role model and as a metaphor for reality. Any analysis of religion as practiced in the modern world must raise these questions, whether or not the conclusions of the psychologists mentioned above are accepted or not. In recent times the work of Will Herberg has demonstrated the profound insights which can come from a theological awareness of these issues. Herberg's study of American religion has revealed in its conception of God, man, and the American people a psychological and sociological use of theology which traditional approaches leave untouched. Herberg himself pioneered a new theological technique which developed its system on the basis of a social-psychological analysis of religious categories and their usage.[34a]

The thinkers we are studying reflect much of the background against which Herberg was writing. Yet the "ecumenical perspective" differs from his sense of "the American Way of Life." It looks for a new theological option which is neither traditional Judaism or Christianity nor the self-serving religiousness of American society in general. Like Herberg they see a prophetic power in authentic "Judeo-Christian Faith." Yet for these thinkers the differences between Judaism and Christianity are transformed by the advocacy of pluralism inherent in the ecumenical perspective. The Hebrew Bible becomes a paradigm through which both the traditional doctrine of Israel's distinctiveness and the psychological insight asserting God's presence as a unifying religious experience are reconciled as equally valid facets of true faith. Looked upon as a document of faith the Bible does indeed seem to have a peculiarity about it. Both Jews and Christians affirm it as the basis of their very different religious traditions. Both Jews and Christians claim that the Bible has come from God and reveals His plan for the world--and yet both communities see that plan in radically different ways.

The shared biblical heritage can become a social metaphor. It can be a symbol of that essential diversity without which religion would stagnate. History inevitably forms a religious community and even holding a scripture in common is no defense against social necessity. The biblical record, however, can also be pressed into service to reveal the underlying unity of the religious experience. Biblical man can be an exemplar pointing the way for all human beings to a meeting with God. The biblical narrative need not be taken in its literal and exclusivist context but may be abstracted from that context as one example of mankind's reaching out for higher horizons. The Bible becomes, on that reading, the record of man's struggle to find a reality beyond that of the social setting, to discover a realm of freedom and personal authenticity. The Bible is witness to the reality of personal truth, to the existence of a level of being that is higher than conditioned history.

For the theologians sharing the ecumenical perspective American theology is reducible to biblical theology. That common base provides the starting point of their theologizing. In this discussion of Jewish theology the biblical issues must be given first priority, focusing on them the dynamic elements of the ecumenical perspective can be brought into clearer view.

The Creative Tension of the Biblical Traditions

Discussions of religious pluralism in America tend to be limited to the relationship between Christian denominations, between Catholics and Protestants, or between Catholics, Protestants, and Jews. While in the abstract other religious traditions may be acknowledged and atheism given a grudging nod, neither are, as William James would say, a "live, forced momentous option." In order to demonstrate the creative interplay to differing religious views, then, it is natural to find Jewish thinkers turning to the relationship between Judaism and Christianity for examples. They claim that the fact that the biblical God can find His home not only in the variety of human experiences recorded in the biblical record itself but also in the diverse cultural heritage of two such distinct traditions testifies to the divine desire for pluralism! Certainly there elements of self-serving ideology in this affirmation. The American Jew can only gain in prestige by associating his status with the dominant Christian community, but the rigor with which Jewish distinctiveness is argued despite the commonality of the biblical heritage is noteworthy.

Robert Gordis finds the pluralism of the Bible a remarkable model for modern living. The vision of the prophets and of the best in the Bible is very appropriate to our times. He describes the messianic expectations of the Bible as the basis for a multi-cultural and multi-ethnic pluralism. When men listen to the voice of these prophets, he claims, they "will turn once more to the development of a living and creative culture, infinite in its variety, color, and form, rooted in the God-given uniqueness of each individual and group."[33] Although modern man has become mass produced, he can overcome this problem by heeding the Bible which will recall for him the importance of diversity and pluralism.

Complicating this situation is the fact that while the social structure is pluralistic, modern man views religion as a single phenomenon. Gordis takes "the proverbial man in the street" very seriously and notes that his religiousness "while undoubtedly suffering from many defects, deserves more of a defense than it has yet received."[34] This religion of the "man in the street" suggests a deeper commonality between religions than institutional variety would lead one to suspect. Such popular religion stresses the common ethical search, love of God, and decent human relations which are conceived of as "the essence of obedience to the divine will, no matter what other creedal and ritual demands the specific tradition may make."[35] Gordis attempts to demonstrate that institutional and popular religion are, in effect, identical. The social institutions of religion serve popular religiosity. Pluralism--conditioned by society--and universal religious values--proclaimed by the popular religious mind-need to be bound together. One attempt at such unification is the development of a universal religion. Gordis looks suspiciously at any such attempt. In the first place such universalism is often a disguise for religious imperialism. Secondly the construction of such an artificial religious expression contradicts social reality:

> To speak of a universal religion, therefore, means to fail to reckon with the complexity of the world and the multiplicity of man's attitudes toward life. What is needed is not deadening uniformity, but fruitful coexistence, based on mutual respect and mutual influence created by keeping open the lines of communication.[36]

Gordis accepts social complexity and the existence of various religious forms. At the same time he wants to argue that these different forms fulfill similar functions. He does this by stressing the role of the individual. He raises the question "where is the will of God to be found among men," and declares "The answer is implicit in biblical thought: it resides only in the conscience of the individual, in the moral will and the intellectual judgment of each human being before his God."[37] The diversity of religious expressions is a framework within which the individual engages in his personal spiritual quest. In a number of ways the individual is best served by institutional pluralism because only a variety of approaches can reinforce the truth that each individual must tread his own path and that within all religious movements, "there are varying and even contradictory emphases, all of which have intrinsic value and which testify, incidentally, that there is no one royal road to the throne of the Most High."[38]

Gordis finds in the biblical view of God, particularly as exemplified in the Judeo-Christian tradition, a symbol of this individualism which also recognizes institutional needs. The ideals and values which Judaism and Christianity share are illumined by their institutional diversity. The heritage of the Bible is interpreted divergently by each religion. This conflicting tradition in the reading of a common scripture means that "each tradition possesses a varying emphasis, a difference in timbre" so that in spite of their commonality each displays "a well-marked individuality."[39] These differences can be productive, Gordis explains. Both commonality and divergency are important elements in a modern religious outlook, and the ways in which the Bible and its theology are used in Judaism and Christianity illustrate just what is needed: "an understanding of the elements of identity and similarity on the one hand, and of difference and opposition on the other."[40] The Judeo-Christian tradition provides a foundation so that men can talk to one another; it produces "a consensus of outlook without which a viable society cannot be maintained," while the institutional separation between Judaism and Christianity creates "the conditions for a fruitful and stimulating dialogue on the perennial issues of God, man and the Universe."[41] Gordis can speak of the need for Jewish-Christian dialogue and suggests that "the concept of the Judeo-Christian tradition takes on genuine relevance in our day" because he is commited to the idea that "no one tradition has all the answers to the mystery of existence and to the challenge of the human condition."[42] God serves neither to legitimate Jewish existence or human potential. His incomprehensibility and infinity function rather to legitimate pluralism and His relevance to the individual, Gordis implies, comes from the moral and ethical values which the religious search inculcates. The ecumenical perspective has integrated belief in God with its perception of the "real world", a world composed of social consciousness and the individual's autonomous search for inner reality.

Jacob Agus uses arguments similar to Gordis but focuses more intently on the individual. The idea of God, he suggests, symbolizes the basic goals of human life. Life, however, is complex and only a complex view of God can do justice to it:

> Our ideas must correspond to life if they are to serve effectively as the goals of life. God is the ultimate Being, in whom three quests

> converge--all of them infinite--the quest for reality, the quest for the realization of goodness, and for the integration of our self with the all-embracing harmony.[43]

The individual needs to be challenged so that he does not neglect one aspect of life because he is so involved in another. To be religious implies an awareness of the depth and breadth of existence. The religious man, Agus suggests, is more alive to the infinite possibilities of life than are others. To be a man of faith, he claims, means to affirm:

> the tension and turmoil of several dialogues --those between faith and reason, between ethnocentrism and universalism, between the humanistic perspective and that of a parochial tradition, between our diverse and apparently contradictory visions of God.[44]

As with Gordis, so too Agus sees the dialogue between the Jewish and Christian views of God particularly relevant in evolving a religious awareness of diversity. Because they represent polar opposites who share similar theological assumptions, Agus finds that Judaism and Christianity challenge one another's mythologies. Institutions are for Agus, as for Gordis, the framework of a personal religious quest. He insists that this framework must always be transcended. Religion always runs the danger of stagnation. He finds the institutions of religion "the instruments of this quest" for human meaning and admits that "Sometimes these instruments work effectively, bringing people to a fresh confrontation of inner or outer reality; sometimes these instruments merely record the vast momentum of the past."[45] The effectiveness of the Judeo-Christian dialogue is that the institutions are always stimulated to act as effective instruments for the individual person. "Genuine religion," Agus comments, "must be aided to retain its dynamism, utilizing myths and transcending them at one and the same time."[46] The biblical view of God is too broad to be contained in any one dogmatic tradition. The existence of two communities whose diversity is based upon an identical scripture points to this truth. Religious man's personal quest gains in importance when this truth is realized; his demand for unity of self is combined with a recognition of life's complexity. Because the Judeo-Christian tradition helps make transparent that God's image is exceedingly complicated, Agus calls on religious men "to welcome the challenge of differences in religion as the stimulus needed to keep faith alive and fresh."[47]

Together with Robert Gordis, Jacob Agus represents one way in which the ecumenical perspective transformed the Jewish perception of God and theology. Although their specific theologies differ, Agus and Gordis share a functionally identical perspective: God is a concept that indicates the diversity of human religiousness and the inner quest for personal reality. It is this functional use of the God-concept which is utilized by theologians exhibiting the ecumenical perspective.

Abraham Heschel's Biblical Theology

While Gordis and Agus used the implied duality in the term "Judeo-Christian tradition" to point out the creative diversity in modern society, Abraham Heschel saw that diversity as a problem to be solved. The biblical God helps man utilize social conditions creatively not because He symbolizes infinite variety but because He shows the way to unity through inner exploration despite that variety. Heschel takes it as an established fact that "In our own age we have been forced into the realization that, in terms of human relations, there will be either one world or no world."[48] No less than Agus and Gordis, Heschel realizes that social structures cannot be depended upon to forge that unity. The civil context is only an arean in which the contest between unity and divisiveness is held. "Political and moral unity as a goal," Heschel argues, "presupposes unity as a source; the brotherhood of men would be an empty dream without the fatherhood of God."[49] The Bible helps modern man precisely because it escapes the social trap. For Heschel the biblical approach to God leads through the inner road of the self and the outer reaches of transcendent existence--avoiding the pitfalls of depending upon social structure. To theologize, for him, is not to advance a concept of deity but to share an insight about reality. The experience of the divine is the reception of "a message that discloses unity where we see diversity, that discloses peace when we are involved in discord."[50]

God, as symbol (although Heschel would eschew that term), functions to provide a glimpse of the social reality of unity which underlies the social structure of diversity. Heschel is uncomfortable with words like "symbol", or "function" because they are derived from social science; they imply that man is utilizing God. God is not, Heschel claims, a thing to be used but a presence to which we respond. At the same time Heschel offers certain criteria for judging whether an experience is truly religious. In these passages we cannot help but be reminded of the psychologists we looked at above. The vision of God does indeed serve an important service--it imbues human life with an ideal of unity which, at least Heschel thinks, cannot be discovered in any other way:

> When God becomes our form of thinking we begin to sense all men in one man, the whole world in a grain of sand, eternity in a moment . . . If in the afterglow of a religious insight I can see a way to gather up my scattered life, to unite what lies in strife; a way that is good for all men as it is for me--I will know it is His way.[51]

Man tests good and evil by testing for unity. Heschel argues that morality consists of supporting the forces of union. By turning to God, to the "source" as Heschel designates Him, the individual finds a unity that has no earthly counterpart. Discovering God, man also discovers a moral task--that of realizing that transcendent vision in everyday life. Morality is not found by looking out at society but by looking upward at God. The similarity between this view and that advanced by certain psychologists noted above is striking. Even Heschel's statement that "evil is *divergence,* confusion, that which *alienates* man from man, man from God, while good is *convergence,* togetherness, union,"[52] reminds us of their views.

We noticed that these thinkers also stressed the duality in man and God, the need to struggle against one's darker self and even use one's darker nature for productive purposes. Heschel, despite his antipathy to psychology, follows just the program they outline. His discussion of man's inner qualities emphasizes that human life "consists of needs as a house consists of bricks . . . "[53] He goes on to note that we are often confused by our needs; we lack a system of priorities. We must learn, he suggests, "how to deal with needs."[54] God's nature teaches us just that lesson. Being in God's image man can model himself on the divine. The divine example enables man to see that "every moment is an extraordinary occasion," in effect, it is an opportunity to be like God. Utilizing this theology Heschel can affirm all human acts and impulses and gives them their place within a divine scheme. God is emblematic of man's ultimate goal--the unification of his nature and the ordering of his needs. God's existence is a model not just for individual life, but for social involvement as well. The unity of God, the divine embracing of all life, can become a metaphor for social life no less than for personal life. Judaism, according to Heschel, "is a theology of the common deed," which teaches man "to attune the comparative to the absolute, to associate the detail with the whole, to adapt our own being with its plurality, conflicts and contradictions to the all-embracing unity, to the holy."[56] Heschel does not shirk the ecumenical responsibility of legitimating the social structure. But its legitimation comes from outside of itself. The social body is not justified because it achieves some end--stimulating complexity, for example--but because it is an opportunity for sanctification. The dual aspect of the ecumenical perspective which was operative in the writings of

Gordis and Agus is also present in Heschel. God unifies men at the depth level--for Heschel that means when human beings are attuned to God they see their intrinsic relationship to all reality--and God justifies a diversified social setting--for Heschel that means that God's unity transforms every particular being into the raw material of divinity.

More themes are present in Heschel, Gordis, and Agus than the two elements of unity and complexity. All three thinkers are struggling with modern man's rejection of ancient myths, his restlessness with traditional metaphors. Perhaps, it might be argued, the supposed commonality between these thinkers is nothing else than the common modernity that they share. To investigate whether it is in fact modernity or the ecumenical perspective that is at stake here we will turn our attention to the thought of Mordecai Kaplan. Kaplan was in the center of American efforts to modernize Jewish thought. He neither sought to replace old metaphors entirely nor merely to refurbish older forms. He offered a "transvaluation" of traditional Jewish language which invested traditional terms with modern meanings. Kaplan, however, did not embrace the ecumenical perspective, so his theology may be productively compared and contrasted with those of the three thinkers studied above.

Themes in Mordecai Kaplan's Theology

At first glance Mordecai Kaplan's notion of God seems clear and straightforward: God is the name given to those forces within man and outside of him that support human self-fulfillment, or in Kaplan's language, salvation. God is a term used to designate those conditions which permit man to achieve selfhood. At the same time Kaplan wants to call God a "process" inherent in the universe, a reality that transcends its component parts as an independent entity. God can be described, perhaps, as the tendency towards human self-actualization which these various forces represent.[57] Scholars and critics have pointed to Kaplan's inconsistencies, to the lack of rigor with which he propounds his theories, to the absence of a clear philosophical position.[58] The present study will not seek to criticize Kaplan anew or to establish his philosophical coherence. Instead it will focus on those concerns which Kaplan shares with theologians reflecting the "ecumenical perspective." Despite these shared concerns we will note the formative power of the myth of ecumenism and how it divides Kaplan from the others. Three basic issues unify all four thinkers. The underlying theme is that of unity but it is expressed through a theology composed of an emphasis on a sense of human potential, a recognition of human weakness and the contention that an awareness of Israel's God helps unify these conflicting elements within society and individuals.

The theme of unity is the predominant one which binds these thinkers together and so it is not out of place to look for it in Kaplan. To focus on this one image may be to distort the range and scope of Kaplan's work. The richness and texture of his thought arises from the wealth of suggestive and stimulating ideas he proposes. To some extent, then, we may be unfair to the breadth of his work, but his influence on the modern theological myth came as much from isolated stimulii hidden in his writings as from his total system.

Some scholars would suggest that it is futile to look for the theme of unity in Kaplan since "The truth is that relying completely on naturalistic experience as Reconstructionism does, one has no possibility of discovering the unity of all reality."[59] We, however, are concerned with mythology, with the images and ideals of a theologian and not with the logic of his argument. Although one might well deny Kaplan the right to affirm unity on the basis of his principles, the fact is that he does. It is this affirmation, particularly in the face of what many would consider powerful counterarguments, which reveals his participation in the construction of the modern Jewish theological myth.

The very notion of God, Kaplan suggests, arises from an intuition of cosmic unity. Man lives in a world of conflict and disorder. His normal experiences are of divergencies, disharmony, discord. Now and again, however, man attains "the intuitive experience of cosmic Power upon which we depend for our existence and self-fulfillment."[60] Men have, he claims, in fact experienced the fact "that the world is governed by a Power that does provide for man whatever is necessary to make life worthwhile for him" and this is the foundation of religious belief.[61] As a functionalist who judges beliefs by the tasks they perform Kaplan feels impelled to ask what difference this belief makes in human life. His answer is that this belief enables man to see the world as an organic whole and to interact with it as such. God signifies "all the relationships, tendencies and agencies which in their totality go to make human life worthwhile in the deepest and most abiding sense."[62] The intuition of God is more than the recognition of this or that force or event which helps fulfill our needs. It is the perception of a pattern, a uniform tendency at work. Life, not merely this or that moment, is significant in its entirety:

> . . . it is only as the sum of everything in the world that renders life significant and worthwhile--or holy--that God can be worshiped by man. Godhood can have no meaning for us apart from human ideals of truth, goodness, and beauty, interwoven in a pattern of holiness."[63]

God represents a sensed unity between diverse events; an intuited coherence of human experience. Belief in God is nothing less for Kaplan than "to reckon with life's creative forces, tendencies and potentialities as forming an organic unity."[64] To perceive God is to recognize and acknowledge this unity in the world.

Such a recognition of a unified tendency for human development is a fitting foundation for man's dignity of selfhood. Without such an intuition, Kaplan claims one must pay a dire penalty: "the failure to reach the conviction of life's true worth."[65] Having perceived this Power making for salvation, however, man finds himself impelled to work together with it. Human beings are the active partner, harnassing and directing the divine forces. The very purpose of seeking God is that of identifying "the particular human experiences which enable us to feel the impact of that process in the environment and in ourselves which impels us to grow and improve physically, mentally, morally, and spiritually."[66] As the agent of change and development working within that process which Kaplan names God, man is a necessary part of creation. Kaplan points out, much in the same way as Heschel, that "God to be God, needs not only the world but also man . . . religion is not an answer to an intellectual need but to man's need to be needed."[67] By being the focus of God's activities man's status is assured; by being the active agent of God's process, man's involvement is also stimulated.

Balancing this optimistic view of man with a realistic assessment of what human beings do in fact achieve, Kaplan uses the idea of God as a check on waywardness. Man can depend on God, but only "if he conforms with the required conditions which constitute the laws of God."[68] While there is within the world a tendency toward good, Kaplan hastens to add that good is a goal not yet achieved. By defining God as a process Kaplan suggests that much remains to be changed. Kaplan notes that the "attitude which encourages man to share the perogative with God must be controlled" since man's creative force is productive only when it manifests "that Power (which) brings order out of chaos and good out of actual and potential evil."[69] If God is to provide a model for human action then He must push man beyond the status quo.

Like Heschel, Gordis, and Agus, Kaplan finds the present situation to be marked by confusion. Good and evil, positive and negative drives, progress and regression characterize modern life. Like these other theologians he offers a view of God to provide unity. "The resolution of inner conflict," Kaplan writes, "demands a faith that identifies the very spirit of revolt against existing conditions with the divinely creative forces in the universe."[70] His interpretation of the deity does just that. It represents a tendency towards unification, a process through which the world and men are transforming themselves. Like Agus and Gordis, Kaplan finds the biblical view of God functional in helping modern man live in a complex environment. Together with Heschel, Kaplan sees the God concept as a symbol of the ideal vision towards which man strives.

These common elements linking Kaplan with the representatives of the ecumenical perspective only underscore his essential difference from them. Kaplan shows no interest in using theology to join religion together. He does not seek to justify religious pluralism nor support the structures of religious institutions. God, as the force for human salvation, is certainly present in these institutions, but Kaplan decidedly ignores that aspect of his theory. His view of God is not explicitly used to endorse and cultivate diversity of religious expressions. Even more explicitly Kaplan denies the relevance of Judaism and the Jewish idea of God for non-Jews. "The relation of one religion to another," he comments, "is like the relation of one mind to another. It is a relation of otherness."[71] The relevance of this view is found in Kaplan's expansion of the concept of God. For Gordis and Agus the concept is related to the biblical tradition and those ideals and values which are derived from it. Creative interaction between Judaism and Christianity on this theological level supports the social structure of pluralism. Kaplan finds God's presence in the totality of life experiences--social structure, individual personality, natural forces, all represent God's presence. Such a conception blurs the very concrete realization of the social setting that Agus and Gordis develop. Their theology focuses on the specific function of God as a social force; Kaplan's includes social life but obscures the social consciousness by relegating social organization to the role of only one element in a total configuration. He is far from a social determinist and seems to use social life, nature, and psychology in a homiletical way as illustrations of what he considers to be "life's basic meaning."

Just as one cannot ascribe the social consciousness to Kaplan one must also deny him the mystical, psychological consciousness which Heschel possesses. While sensitive to the same moral and ethical issues as Heschel, Kaplan does not see the biblical God as such the primary focus for inner search and transcendent visions. The experience of unity, which for Heschel is a confrontation with transcendent reality, becomes for Kaplan an intuition, a scientific hypothesis, based upon the data of everyday life. While Heschel claims that religion enables us to look beyond the reality given us in mundane life, Kaplan claims that religion is a synthesis of just that reality. The psychological awareness of man's inner life, the depth reality of human consciousness, animates Heschel's exposition of theology. Without this consciousness Kaplan is left to discover unity within empirical experience. It is difficult to see how Kaplan would overcome the obstacle of comparative social studies. The empirical experience of different human communities should yield different generalizations. Kaplan is not concerned with this possibility because comparative studies do not interest him. Without the ecumenical perspective he finds no need to discern a depth-human consciousness uniting disparate populations. While his sensitivity to modernity joined him with Heschel in an ethical concern, his rejection of ecumenism helped distinguish his theological approach from that of his other colleagues.

The Myth of Religious Man and the Ecumenical Perspective

How has the ecumenical perspective shaped Jewish theology? Certainly Gordis and Agus are theologically distinguishable and Heschel is just as definitely an independent thinker. Yet all three have a conception of religious man and his task in the modern world which binds them together. This conception can be called the "myth of religious man" because it consists of a projected image of an ideal person. The idea of God which religious man bears in modern life, according to these thinkers, plays an important role in transforming social and private life. On one level religious man is a promethean figure whose consciousness of God brings a new dimension to human life. The social setting with its pluralism and religious diversity gains from this gift. Religious man strides through society, as Agus and Gordis see it, proclaiming new and different truths and challenging all efforts to reduce man's conception of deity to a single, simple-minded view. The social consciousness which is associated with the ecumenical perspective becomes a vital force in theology. God's infinite nature becomes religious man's justification for diversity of institutional religious groups.

A second element in the ecumenical shaping of Jewish theology derives from psychological awareness. While promethean in his challenge to society religious man is also Job-like in his self-centered search for inwardness. Heschel finds religious man looking beyond social life to a transcendent reality. Social ills are many, evil is prevalent, but the transcendent vision provided by the symbol "God" gives religious man his strength. To effectively challenge uniformity religious man must be rooted in a specific, parochial tradition. To intuit the unity behind diversity religious man needs the assurance given by a vision of inner reality. This vision cannot be associated with any one tradition but is a universally human one. Self-acceptance, in these terms, means acceptance of humanity and the human lot. Maurice Friedman has explored the ways in which modern thinkers have tended to emphasize one or the other of these roles--the promethean or the joban. He concludes that both are necessary stages in modern man's religious development.[72] Heschel's approach is, thus, the necessary complement of that found in Agus and Gordis.

The purpose of our investigation has been to point out how the ecumenical perspective shaped a new myth of Jewish religion. The idea of God became a talisman by which the modern Jew could affirm social pluralism and individual existential religious meaning. While sociologists will point out other elements in their work--a focus on individualism, a concern for unity and coherence, a deep ethical concern--we want to suggest the mythological power in their theologies. The realities of modernity cannot be denied--Kaplan saw and reacted to them no less than Agus, Gordis and Heschel. Religion, however, is intriguing just because it augments reality with a mythology of reality. Agus, Heschel, and Gordis do this by positing both a divine sanction and participation in religious pluralism and a divinely transmitted vision of ultimate unity. In constructing a myth of God's nature and His role in modern life these thinkers converted the social consciousness of a world structured by diverse social institutions into an affirmation of divine infinitude. They transformed their perception of man's internal reality into a vision of God's transcendent unity. Here we find the most important effect of the ecumenical perspective. It enabled a mythologization of the two modern approaches to life--the sociological and the psychological-mystical. Modern man's perception of reality is converted into a religious message by means of theology. God as the symbol of social pluralism and the intuition of a basic human vision of the transcendent functions to lift modern perceptions of life into the realm of the eternal. Modern men see the world as they do, this mythology suggests, not merely because of the conditions of our life but because these perspectives are part of an enduring divine consciousness. What do we learn from this? Human beings are often uncomfortable with their bare perceptions of reality. They seek to root these views of life in a larger framework. The ecumenical perspective proceeded to provide that framework for two modern ways of understanding the world. These theologians adjust to modernity by transforming it. Modernity is not, for them, merely the context of everyday life. Unlike Kaplan they refuse to take modernity at its secularist word. They elevate it by means of the ecumenical perspective so that God's concern with social diversity and with the individual's exploration of transcendent reality becomes a way of sanctifying modern consciousness.

CHAPTER III

RITUAL AS ENACTMENT OF THE THEOLOGICAL MYTH

Traditional Rituals and Modernity

The theological myth of the ecumenical perspective differs, as we have seen, from traditional Jewish thinking. The intimate relationship between myth and ritual would lead us to expect a change in Jewish ritual behavior corresponding to the mythological transformations noted previously. In fact sociologists have noted the untraditional nature of American Jewish ritual patterns. Marshall Sklare, for example, contending that Judaism is a "sacramental" religion of which ritual practice is the central reality finds in the transformation of ritual observance an important indication of the pressures of Americanism and modernity.[73] Sklare discovers an inherent contradiction between the norms of Jewish tradition and those of modernity: traditionally ritualism was legitimated by "criteria internal to the religious system," but in the modern world private meaning has become the most essential criterion. In developing a ritualism based upon personal criteria rather than traditional ones "the tenets that were hallowed in traditional life may conflict sharply with contemporary culture, and those that were formerly of secondary importance may achieve primacy because they fulfill important needs."[74] The survey data to which Sklare turns supports his contention that Jewish ritualism has been transformed in the modern world. Further support is added by comparing Sklare's findings with Charles Liebman's study of the "religion of American Jews," which also suggests that contemporary Jewish practice follows a deviant pattern from that established by traditional Judaism.[75]

The model normally used to explain this deviant ritualism is that of accommodation to the non-Jewish world.

Sklare suggests that by remolding tradition to fit the modern environment the Jewish elite hoped to stimulate increased observance. Paraphrasing the Jewish liturgy, Sklate summarized this effort as the belief that "liberalization--in combination with innovation and beautification--will succeed in averting the evil decrees of non-observance."[76] Such an explanation may hold true for the ritualism of many Jewish thinkers, but it is inadequate as a model for understanding the role of ritual in the ecumenical perspective. The adjustment of ritual to meet the needs of modernity was less an end in itself for advocates of this view than a means by which the twin realities of the social construction of the world and the personal space of inner life could be symbolized and evoked in consciousness. Ritualism becomes a vehicle for the establishment and preservation of both pluralism and the depth-dimension of faith. Judaism's particular practices are interpreted as parts of a wider system of religious symbolism; they represent one alternative route to the universal religious goal.

Perceiving ritual in this way means seeing it to some extent as "civil religion"--as a legitimation and justification of the general community as well as of the specific Jewish culture. Jewish practice is profoundly important as a contribution to civil society as well as being a depth-experience for the individual. The concept of a civil ritual, however, may develop independently of the ecumenical perspective. While a sense of ritual's civil role does evolve from the dual commitment to pluralism and personalism it is not limited to this source for its power. Mordecai Kaplan concerned himself with developing an American civil ritualism and supported his theories with a variety of practical suggestions. Unlike theologians sharing the ecumenical perspective, however, Kaplan sought to create a new ritual system that might coexist with the independent religious traditions. While Agus, Gordis, and Heschel might agree with Kaplan that all Americans are united in a common religious experience they would disagree that this unity cannot be legitimated and expressed through the particularistic cults of each individual religious group. This difference in evaluation of the expressiveness of particularistic rituals needs to be explored as one key to the way in which the ecumenical perspective conceived of ritualism.

Before turning to the specific theories of the theologians involved it may be helpful to consider some general issues raised by the religious practice of ritual. Two such issues will be of central concern here: what is the function of ritual and how does one interpret the secularization of ritual practice. The discussion of the function rituals play is a controversial one. Some writers reduce the meaning of ritual to one or another of its functions--ritual can be seen as a means of coping with individual frustrations, of binding the individual to the social group, of producing social solidarity. Rather than follow the lead of any one of these approaches and reduce religious ritual to another aspect of human life, other scholars argue for rituals as intrinsically meaningful, as transparent symbols for a reality that cannot be indicated in any other way. Such "symbolic realism" takes ritual on its own terms and treats it as a unique religious phenomenon. Both views, however, share a common approach to the decoding of rituals: they point beyond themselves and indicate a reality present in the lives of their followers. This reality may be a social or psychological one or it might be a transcendental one. While divided on the issue of the reality to which it points, these analysts do seem to agree that ritualism is indicative in function.

Another function of ritual, however, is far more problematic--its cognitive function. If rituals do more than indicate a reality and transmit a definite cognitive message, then they must be taken seriously as a source of human knowledge. The popular conception of symbolism and ritual makes this cognitive function seem unlikely. Most modern symbols are too ambiguous and multi-valenced to convey direct meaning; modern rituals are too often so personal in content that they cannot be decoded into a communicable message.[77] Yet scholars like Mircea Eliade contend that "The symbol reveals certain aspects of reality--the deepest aspects--which defy any other means of knowledge."[78] If the theologians sharing the ecumenical perspective make the claim that Jewish ritualism conveys not merely an indication of reality but a message about reality, a cognition of truth, then they do have a traditional scholarly support behind them. That support comes not from common experience, however, but from analysts like Eliade who work in decoding religious traditions far from those of modern man.

Here is a particularly clear example of how the ecumenical perspective finds itself confronting modernity. Regarding ritual through either the social scientific or personalist consciousness theologians inevitably must confront social or psychological reductionism. Both ways of constructing reality subject rituals and symbols to what Gilbert Cope calls "the assault direct . . . the exhaustive analysis of symbols and of *symbolism* also tends to reduce their efficacy."[79] Modern rituals must confront a new dilemma--that of functioning in world-views that are detrimental to the ritual process itself. As Mary Douglas points out, once rituals function for an extrinsic purpose "Why celebrate at all? As soon as symbolic action is denied value in its own right the floodgates of confusion are opened."[80] The definitions of cognition and truth provided by the social scientific and personalist consciousness seems inimical to the power of ritualism. The ecumenical perspective and its representatives confront an inner tension in their efforts to modernize Jewish ritual by translating it into the new consciousness.

All efforts to secularize or reduce religious ritual to terms other than intrinsically religious ones need not be seen as "modernization." Although such a conflict is part of the modern problem it is not exclusively modern. Mary Douglas herself has pointed out that the rejection of ritual as intrinsically meaningful "is not essentially a product of the city. There are secular tribal societies."[81] Merely finding the abandonment of certain rituals, acculturation or assimilation of non-religious values, and revisions of ritual practices does not inevitably mean modernization. Certainly Mordecai Kaplan's thinking is radically non-traditional, and yet we will find that it does not fit the model of modernity and modernization which lies at the base of the ecumenical perspective. Secularization and the decline of supernaturalism is not necessarily a sign of religious decline, of radical religious self-transformation. Religious changes can often be perceived by those making them as completely compatible with and continuous with tradition. Shlomo Deshen has studied religion in the State of Israel and denies that certain ritualistic changes are in fact "secular" and "modern." On the basis of his studies he concludes that there is a fundamental difference between transformations of ritual and religious modernization. Therefore he opposes the use of "secularization" as a basic term to describe ritual changes. The rigid polarity between traditional ritual and secularized religion seems false to him. "Change in religious practices," he notes, "can be rooted in casuistic mechanisms inherent in canon law to enable change; the same changes can sometimes be devoid of such traditional control and legitimization."[82] Even the abandonment of certain symbols or practices are not, he argues, unambiguous signs of secularization. They may often be manifestations of a deep commitment to traditional religious faith.[83] When he studies specific innovations in custom and Jewish law practiced by immigrants to Israel, Deshen stresses that those who practice them do so because they desire to express conventional religious feelings. "In all these instances," he comments, "the new experimental content infused into the symbolic action molds the action into a particular form and direction without excluding the old experiential content."[84]

As we look at theologians who contend with modernity we should be sensitive to their self-image. Do they consider themselves as making a radical break with the past? Are they self-consciously rejecting an older ritual experience? Or might they be, at least in their own eyes, continuing the tradition by the innovations they introduce? Does their sense of self-alienation or sense of continuity bear a relationship to the ecumenical perspective? We will try to find out whether such a pattern of relationships exists that would find important differences in self-perception connected with acceptance or rejection of the ecumenical perspective.

The Problem of Jewish Ritual: Personal Faith or Social Relevance?

Jewish theologians never questioned the assumption that Jewish ritualism was in trouble. Not merely Mordecai Kaplan and Abraham Heschel, Jacob Agus and Robert Gordis who are being singled out here as articulate representatives, but the audiences of rabbis and thinkers they addressed never once challenged their analysis of Jewish ritual as in crisis. The responses to their work are varied, but they concentrate on the way the problem is construed or on the specific answers given and not on the fact that there is a problem. Our first concern, then, will not be to prove or disprove whether Jewish ritualism needs revitalization; it can be assumed that at least among the religious elite such a need was perceived as real. Instead we should ask how that problem was conceived, what some of the reasons for the state of American Jewish ritualism were thought to be. An instructive beginning to this investigation is an acrimonious session of the 1953 annual convention of the Rabbinical Assembly of America (the organization of Conservative Rabbis and with which each of the four thinkers studied is associated). The session was called together to discuss the modern significance of Jewish ritual and the speakers were selected, as one participant put it, "with malice aforethought," so that two contrasting views could illuminate one another. Abraham Joshua Heschel gave the first address on "The Spirit of Prayer," followed by another talk on the same subject by Eugene Kohn, a disciple of Mordecai Kaplan and an exponent of Reconstructionist thought. A full discussion ensued upon the completion of the talks and responses by the speakers then concluded the sessions.[85] Heschel spoke as an adversary of those who thought ritual could be modernized through innovation and prayerbook reform. The idea of bringing the Jewish view of God "up to date" repelled him. He offered an alternative approach of modernizing by strengthening the spiritual appeal of Jewish ritual and demonstrating its potential as a liberation from technological domination. Drawing upon the insights of Eastern European Hasidism he characterized prayer as a means "to overcome that predicament" which plaques modern man, it is a means "to see the world in a different setting." "There are," he continues, "bitter problems which religion has to solve: agony, sin, despair."[86] Prayer is in crisis because religion is in crisis, because the inner man has been neglected. "The trouble with the prayerbook," Heschel proclaims, "is: it is too great for us, it is too lofty . . . our souls are often lost in its sublime wilderness."[87] His approach to ritual decried any attempt to realign tradition to modern deficiencies. Modern man must be taught to see ritual as a challenge to his inwardness, as a demand for personal response. "The problem," he argued, "is not how to revitalize prayer; the problem is how to revitalize ourselves."[88] Ritual is as much a diagnostic test as it is a solution. It reveals the spiritual bankruptcy of modern life. The experience of ritual living is one of inner discovery and of contact with a divine power beyond oneself. Through that experience horizons are widened, the ego expands to recognize the non-ego, life is placed into a universal perspective. We have difficulties with prayer, Heschel suggests, because we have lost spiritual insight and are locked into a self-centered world.

Heschel's use of ritual as a challenge to modern man and his social context evoked a sharp reaction. It was charged that "his characterization of the American synagogue was unworthy."[89] The second talk by Eugene Kohn gave a summary of the Reconstructionist approach to ritual. Since the views of Mordecai Kaplan will be discussed in detail later the remarks of his disciple need only be summarized here so that the sharp distinction between his concerns and those of Heschel is made clear. Kohn stressed the sociological and intellectual realities of American Jewish life and noted the discontinuity between them and Jewish life in Eastern Europe. To be effective a Jewish liturgy would need to reflect American realities and not Hasidic fantasies. Such a liturgy should reflect a more mature concept of God derived from social science and should begin to employ concepts and symbols prominent in American civil experience. An infusion of indigenous religious content can revitalize the meaning of Jewish ritual while the alien meaning system derived from Eastern Europe addresses Americans in an incomprehensible foreign language. Only a reform of Jewish ritual which takes account of the challenges which modern philosophy, sociology, and psychology have made on the ancient pattern of symbolic behavior has a chance of success. Modern man, he admitted, needs a powerful set of symbols but none is available to him--either from tradition or from the secular world. The task of the religious leader, Kohn suggests, is to create a new ritualism which would fill the gap created by modernity.[90]

In this exchange between Heschel and Kohn we find that both thinkers agree on one point: Jewish ritual does not make contact with the modern Jew. For Heschel this lack of contact is a symptom of an inner disease. Jews need ritual to recognize how ill they really are. By revealing the depth of modern man's condition Jewish ritual helps reorient him to those inner needs and transcendent expectations which are being neglected. Kaplan and Kohn, his disciple, locate the problem within ritual itself. Jewish ritual does not communicate with modern man because it uses an antiquated language and an incomprehensible symbol system. To restore ritual's significance it must be translated into a new idiom. Heschel seeks to revive ritual by reviving modern man; Kaplan and his followers contend that only a revived ritualism reconstructed to be meaningful in a modern context can revive the modern Jew.

Heschel's argument claims that only by exposing himself to traditional Jewish ritual can the modern Jew revitalize his life. He is joined in this claim by others including Robert Gordis who find in traditional Jewish practice an intrinsically powerful instrument for molding human life. The full set of Jewish observances in its original form is conceived of as an independent spiritual entity which can effect substantial changes in a person's sense of self. There is an intrinsic worthwhileness in Jewish ritual, both Heschel and Gordis submit, which reaches beyond its pragmatic benefits of health, happiness, or communal spirit.[91]

The basis for this claim is the supposition that the ritual moment is shared with God; the foundation of ritual is its power to provide opportunities for self-transcendence. As Gordis characterizes it, ritual is essentially "an act of communion that man establishes with God."[92] The law of God, the practices He enjoins, are seen as "min hashamayim"--from heaven--because they represent the possibility of men joining God in the performance of a religious act. The Hebrew term for such an act is *mitzvah* or commandment. Heschel expands the meaning of this term so that it refers not only to the traditional religious expectations of the Judaic system but to any act which affirms transcendence:

> A mitzvah is an act which God and man *have*

> *in common*. . . . The destiny of man is to be a partner of God and a mitzvah is an act in which man is present, an act of participation . . . A mitzvah is an act in which we go beyond the scope of our thought and intention.[93]

This stress on ritual's opportunity to grow beyond oneself and to share a moment with God is crucial; it permits Heschel and Gordis to allow certain practical changes in observance while stressing the intrinsic holiness of the entire ritual pattern. Since each particular ritual is an opportunity in itself, the modern Jew who cannot accept the entire system of observances can be urged to avail himself to whatever ritual he can. Jewish legalism, the argument runs, flourished in a particular environment; although that environment no longer exists, we can utilize mitzvot as ways of intuiting the divine even if we must reduce the quantitative frequency of their performance. Heschel admits:

> The industrial civilization has profoundly affected the condition of man, and vast numbers of Jews loyal to Jewish law feel that many of the rabbinic restrictions tend to impede rather than to inspire joy and love of God. . . . The power to observe depends on the situation.[94]

In the modern situation it is possible to tolerate a reduction in observance. What it is impossible to tolerate is a reduction of the concept of mitzvah to imply social or psychological utilitarianism. Gordis notes that ritual observance has declined and that "the practices which are being retained or revived tend to be those which are unique and non-repetitive in life . . . This is insufficient for a religiously committed Jew, but it is a starting point."[95] Recognizing each ritual as an opportunity of its own both Gordis and Heschel are flexible enough to applaud the "starting place" of minimalism.

Such an approach enables these thinkers to retain a traditionalist view of ritual while responding to unmistakeable social needs. The transcendental uniqueness of each commandment is affirmed; the traditional form of observance is the special spiritual instrument by which modern man learns to know his own needs. But one need not insist on total observance, on obedience to the entire scope of Jewish law. Heschel advocates a "ladder of observances" to permit the individual to move from lower levels of faith--relatively few moments shared with God--to higher levels. Each mitzvah represents a concentrated, intense experience in its full traditional meaning. But as man moves from minimal to maximal exposure to these moments he revives "the sense of divine relevance of human deeds, the affirmation of man's kinship with God."[96] These infrequent experiences are social in consequence even if they are personal and private in essence. Acceptance of minimalism is only one reflection of the social awareness Heschel and Gordis possess. They enumerate the social consequences of the widened scope provided by the ritual experience. Gordis insists that modern man has been trained in passivity and indifference. What we do in our leisure time stamps our entire personalities. Modern recreation is passive and the modern participation in sports is, he claims, that of spectator. The desire to be entertained has replaced the will to create and man's sense of personal responsibility has been undermined. The ritual experience, on the other hand, is active and demands personal response. Man learns that he must be a participant, a co-partner with God and that hours of prayer and ritual are hours of creativity. Ritual corrects the passive, entertainment orientation of American life.[97]

At this point the mythological meaning of ritual is given a modern significance. The traditional statement that ritual moments are moments spent with God is now interpreted to mean that ritual experience redeems man from the trivialization of personal action which characterizes modern life. The step taken seems like a small one. Ritual is an experience of self-transcendence; a free society needs men who recognize the importance of such self-transcendence; ritual is a pre-condition for democracy. As Heschel puts the case the test of ritual is in its ability to transform the person. The performance of a mitzvah is the expression of man's sense that more is asked of him than he realizes. Mitzvot are reminders of social obligation and responsibility because they are experiences of transcendence:

> All mitsvot are means of evoking in us the awareness of living in the neighborhood of God, of living in the holy dimension. They call to mind the inconspicuous mystery of things and acts, and are reminders of our being the stewards, rather than the landlords of the universe . . . The mitsvot are formative. The soul grows by noble deeds. The soul is illumined by sacred acts. Indeed, the purpose of all mitsvot is to refine man.[98]

At this point Heschel merely restates the traditional notion that the meaning of ritual is found in its connection with God and the modern corollary that meeting with God reveals social obligations. He proceeds to remark that society depends upon such moments of insight. A democratic society, he contends, needs people who make decisions based upon a sense of responsibility to others, people who can transcend their own self-interest. Yet where can people learn to become responsive to others? Spiritual resources have been depleted, he continues, older ideologies--socialism, Hebraism, unionism--"which held an earlier generation in their spell, have lost their vitality. This is the hour for the rediscovery of the grandeur of our tradition."[99] The ritual experience is in its essence a meeting with God, an indication of a different realm of existence from everyday life. Participating in such a meeting with the divine, however, man learns a cognitive fact about himself, an anthropological datum as it were: he is able to transcend himself. Ritual provides more than a glimpse at eternity--it assures man that he is capable of rising higher than his baser needs. Heschel insists that modern man requires just this confirmation of his spiritual abilities. The fate of freedom and democracy depend upon man's self-awareness and self-confidence spiritually. "Unless a person learns how to rise daily to a higher plane of living, to care for that which surpasses his immediate needs, "Heschel asks warningly, "will he in a moment of crisis insist upon loyalty to freedom?"[100] Ritual becomes the experience which conditions social man to act for freedom. The transformation of self that occurs in the hidden recesses of the personal world functions to create a new force in the observed social sphere. Ritual provides in this way what Robert Gordis calls "the highway for the penetration of the religious into secular life."[101]

The theory of ritual enunciated here seeks to resolve the tension between ritual and both the social scientific consciousness and personal consciousness. While the ritual function is socially observable and can be interpreted as a necessary social force it cannot be reduced to this because its origins lie in personal life. The personal experience, however, is not merely psychological or private. Ritual provides a true cognition--a new self-knowledge, a confirmation of personal ability. The fluidity with which the influence of ritual performances flows between the private inner world and the observable social world insures both its reality and its comprehensibility to modern man. The same fluidity is present in the ease with which both traditional ritualism and modern concessions are blended in the practical suggestions these theologians make. Traditional Jewish law is upheld since secularism needs precisely the jarring perspective that tradition offers. Gordis suggests, strikingly, that to reconstruct Jewish ritual for the sake of the secular Jew would be like sanctioning theft, murder and rape so that theives, murderers and rapists would feel more at home in America![102] Gordis does not deny that ritual needs revitalization. He encourages new forms of teaching and preaching, new ways of communicating the importance of Jewish ritual. But he insists that respect for Jewish law and stricter observance of it is the only way to effect its resurgence.[103] In short he admits the practical situation and allows for minimalism as the reality but demands that the ideal remain traditional and uncompromised. Heschel argues in a similar way. He too agrees that minimalism is the practical way to begin a revival of Jewish practice. He too agrees that the ideal should remain unchanged. More concretely even than Gordis, however, Heschel affirms the social context and its role in religious life. To revive ritual society itself must be transformed; the environment which conditions men must itself be conditioned. The task of the religiously committed Jew is to restructure the American social atmosphere:

> We should strive to cultivate an atmosphere in which the Jewish form of living is the heartily approved of or at least respected pattern, in which sensitivity to *Kashrut* (dietary laws) is not regarded as treason against the American Constitution.[104]

One cannot help but feel that Gordis and Heschel are making the best of a bad situation. They recognize minimalism--what else would be possible? They justify the social utility of transcendent experience--how else can they appeal to a general audience? As realistic appraisers of the current situation they see the limits beyond which they cannot go. Certainly there is more than a small dose of such opportunism in their writings. Yet what a grandiose mythological encasing is given for their polemic! The image of religious man acting out a cosmic drama every time he engages in a ritual is compelling. The universal significance of man's internal travels in the supernal realm is a profound myth. Its roots in the past, its relationship to ancient Gnosticism or mystical writings, are certainly present. But in a significant way this is a modern myth. Religious man is struggling with the conflict between social and psychological consciousness and attempting to unite them in his being. His unitary vision, informed by a transcendent sense of purpose and obligation, draws strength from an inner reality in order to participate in the technological determinism of his social environment. Ritual moments of spiritual freedom are balanced by the enchained existence of everyday life. Both sides of reality are intrinsic parts of this new myth that informs Jewish ritual.

While the same pragmatic impetus to make the best of a bad situation was at work influencing Mordecai Kaplan and his followers, they proceeded on radically different basic assumptions. True ritual, they contend, is primarily a coded means of communication. Its purpose is educational--to convey certain ideas and values by means of a system of symbols that appeals to the emotions as well as to the mind. The effective and legitimate use of ritualism:

> comes into being when rites and observances are practiced for what they do to stir the mind and the heart religiously. They are a means of enabling man to commune with himself, or with his fellow-men, about things divine.[105]

The revitalization of Jewish ritual entails an effort to re-establish its power to stir the mind and heart. Ritual is to be made more explicitly the carrier of culture. It is to become self-consciously the affirmation of the religious community which "provides . . . a social heritage of language, habits of thought and action, and a sense of values."[106] Ritual is justified not by its expansion of an individual's inner life but by its ability to teach those values and concerns which socialize the individual and bind him to his community. Kaplan does not deny that ritual can "direct and foster the inner drive to fulfill ourselves as human beings."[107] He only urges that this drive be seen as part of a social constellation of moral values. He recognizes that ritual needs to be not merely symbolic in meaning but "the meaning itself has to be such as to activate the better part of us."[108] Like Heschel, Kaplan acknowledges the personal expansion and impetus to self-transcendence which ritual provides. But he denies that this effect derives from an intrinsically powerful external source. Ritual is not an independent reality but "a means of communication concerning states of mind pertaining to God which are regarded as helpful by a number of people."[109] If symbolism and ritual are in trouble it is because there has been a breakdown in communication, a lapse in the "common approval of what those symbols mean."[110] The problem with American Jewish ritual lies in the absense of a consensus on the meaning and value of ritual and symbolism rather than on a lack of personal responsiveness and inner life.

Kaplan complains that the modern non-Jewish environment influenced what he calls "only the Jewish *folk* spirit" and transformed Jewish ritual so that the "average person" (sic!):

> seldom treats religious symbols as symbols which are intended to bring his emotions and his will under control, to help him achieve his full humanity.[111]

American life, in particular, is particularly bankrupt of symbolism and ritual. It is no wonder that Jews are confused about the meaning of their religious rites and ceremonies. American democratic faith has evolved no model of religious symbolism which they could adapt for thier personal religious expression. The crisis in American values is, Kaplan suggests, paralleled by the Jewish ritual crisis. America, he contends, needs a religious sense of destiny and direction. "As Americans, therefore," he comments, "we should identify those experiences and strivings in American life and history which would not only give organic character to the American people, but also set it on the road to human progress and perfection."[112] Because America lacks this national faith--*pace* Robert Bellah, whose writings come after Kaplan--the Jew must move into the forefront of American life and help evolve a new civil ritualism:

> The separation of church from state, with the American people, and of the synagogue from all social agencies, with American Jewry, are portents of a religious crisis. But though crisis spells danger, it also spells opportunity. The present crisis offers American Jewry the opportunity to serve the American people.[113]

There is a double crisis and therefore a double

opportunity. In their particularistic, cultural setting Jews must begin integrating religious and social ideals. Traditional religio-cultural events are interpreted by Kaplan as significant guideposts to social life. The Jewish New Year is explained in terms of Democracy's involvement in world wars; the Festival of Booths entails the same social ideals as the American Declaration of Independence and the Bill of Rights; Passover is an occasion for refuting Karl Marx, defending the American constitution, and discussing the meaning of political liberties.[114]

On another level the Jews must religionize American life. They are to do this by constructing new rituals for civil ceremonies. Kaplan does not see traditional rituals as providing this civil content but rather as providing models for the translation of civil ideals into symbolic language. Once the Jews have become proficient at such translations by restructuring their own ritual traditions they can draw on this experience to develop a new American pattern of celebration. Tutored by their efforts to revitalize Jewish ritual, Jews can turn to what Kaplan designates as their second great task which is "to promulgate an indigenous civic religion for the American people that shall act as a unifying influence, uniting all Americans regardless of race, creed, or status, without being authoritarian or coercive."[115]

Kaplan's realistic assessment of American life should not be taken lightly. Unlike some sociologists he did not contend that America possesses a vital civil faith. He was too aware of the crisis of values, the ambiguity with which all types of ritual activities were viewed to think that Americans have evolved a powerful religious system of their own. He could not have agreed with Robert Bellah that "there actually exists alongside of and rather clearly differentiated from the churches an elaborate and well-institutionalized civil religion in America."[116] He did admit that it might be "possible in America for the various religious and racial groups to meet on common ground," were they to utilize and revitalize a complex of symbols, myths and metaphors "which taken together may be said to constitute the national faith."[117] Still it remained for him and others of the Reconstructionist movement to take those symbols, myths and metaphors together and weld them into a religious statement. To be sure, he recognized certain basic American ideals--freedom, personal self-fulfillment, freedom from absolutism. In themselves these ideals were not yet religious principles. By wedding them to traditional Jewish ritual Kaplan informed them with religious significance.

While one can charge Kaplan, like Heschel, with merely attempting to refurbish Jewish tradition by making it more Americanized, to do so would be to miss an important point. Kaplan is saying more than that Jewish ritual needs to be in tune with American life. He wants Jewish religion to contribute to American faith, to transform American religiousness. Religious ritual does not merely express cultural ideals, it crystalizes and formulates them. Jewish ritual can be an active influence in American life according to Kaplan. Why, then, does he part company with Heschel and emphasize the social dynamics of ritual and symbolism? Kaplan sees the flaw in Jewish ritual to lie in its alien accents. His myth of religious man finds him moving through modernity in such a way that the Jew learns to accustom himself to reality and the American learns to articulate his Americanism. In contrast to Heschel and Gordis, Kaplan finds that ritual permits the modern Jew to feel at home in the world. Whereas Heschel and Gordis see ritual as intrinsically powerful, Kaplan reduces it to a metaphor of culture. The lessons it teaches are not uniquely its own but a symbolic recasting of social values.

Contrasting Kaplan to Heschel and Gordis may be unfair. All of them emphasize continuity with the tradition and stress the ways in which even the radical change they advocate has its roots in the Judaic heritage. Kaplan is more explicit in his desire to break with the past. The symbols and rituals may be retained but Kaplan admits that he has invested them with strikingly untraditional meaning. Jacob Agus, however, exemplifies a more congenial response to Kaplan's approach. He insists that ritual must be changed so that the modern Jew can recognize himself in its image. He was instrumental in drafting a "responsum" or rabbinic decision which legitimated riding to synagogue and using electricity in a synagogue on the Sabbath. When others--among them Robert Gordis--wrote dissenting opinions claiming that tradition could not be served by radical change, Agus responded by defending his position. Tradition's ideal of piety, he claimed, could not be used productively by modern Jews. His efforts at modernization were not motivated by a desire to increase observance of Jewish rituals, he explained. He did hope that the Jew who rode to synagogue on the Sabbath could now turn to the tradition and find himself reflected in its ritual. Rather than be branded as sinner--a self-definition that could only be problematic to someone whose basic motivation for breaking the Sabbath law was a desire to observe the Sabbath ritual--Agus contended that those who drive to synagogue should be commended.[118] Agus, however, holds a more subtle and integrated view of the relationship between the Jew and modern life than does Kaplan. While Kaplan seeks an American ritual that conveys religious values and a Jewish ritual that suggest American ideals, Agus looks for an integrated self-image. His ideal is a synthesis of the standards of society and the vision of tradition. One's sense of purpose and self-definition, he suggests, is created out of both "the objective standards of piety and the good life that derive from the *yetzer tob* (good conscience) of modern thought and civilization" and the subjectively affirmed Jewish heritage.[119] Ritual is seen as an intrinsically powerful element in human life which, however, is balanced by an equally powerful civil culture. Agus, then, joins Heschel and Gordis in an awareness of the interpenetration of conditioned social environment and the free, ethically creative experience of ritual. The effort to unite social and personal realities characterizing Heschel and Gordis is found in Agus as well despite his other affinities to Kaplan.

The Democratization of the Jewish Sabbath

How would a concrete example of the civil implications of a Jewish ritual be constructed? While Kaplan has provided a blueprint for the American civil religion, does the ecumenical perspective offer any equally practical demonstration of the civil relevance of Jewish practice? The way in which the Jewish Sabbath is interpreted demonstrates the unification of social and personal world-views implied in the theological affirmation of pluralism and transcendent unity. Such interpretations stand in contrast to the acculturation model which explains the clearly deviant pattern of Jewish practice on the basis of assimilation. Studies using that model emphasize the role of women and its untraditionality; American religious values have infiltrated Jewish sex models.[120] Unconventional forms of Sabbath practice have made substantial inroads into Jewish homes and have been accepted as standard convention.[121] Some thinkers point to these changes as evidence of acculturation to a new environment. Jews retained only those Sabbath practices "which remained functional from a sociological perspective, within the context of American life."[122] The pattern of Sabbath observance that evolved was democratically constructed--it reflected the American Jew and his concerns rather than imposing the authoritarian religious standards of an external guide. The free spirit of individual religious choice in Sabbath ritualism and legal observances was often displayed immediately upon landing in the new world.[123] In other cases only when ideals--justice, civil rights, pascifism--associated by Jews with American culture conflicted with the restrictions of Jewish law that the Sabbath was abandoned.[124] Using the model of acculturation the Sabbath appears a victim of

American democracy. Jews became religious "American style." Using a basic American ethical code as their guide Jews saw in religiousness only the striving to "be a good person" and Jewish ritual was retained only in so far as it met this culturally determined criterion.[125]

Both representatives of the ecumenical perspective and theologians like Mordecai Kaplan confront the reality of a democratized Sabbath. They cannot help but admit that in American personal choice rather than legal precedent form the basis for Sabbath observance. Yet admitting that reality does not necessarily entail accepting the acculturation model suggested above. Indeed both Kaplan and theologians expressing the ecumenical perspective would insist that a democratized Sabbath is a corrective to and a necessary addition to American cultural life. As we might expect Kaplan argues on the basis of his socio-cultural model of Judaism's coexistence with the American civil religion. Abraham Heschel provides a cogent argument based upon the ecumenical perspective. Kaplan's primary concern is to show that the Sabbath does not contradict American democratic principles and deepens the commitment of the individual Jew to those principles. By practicing his own cultural tradition the Jew, Kaplan wants to say, becomes a better and more productive American.

Heschel's approach is more universalistic in scope. The Sabbath is a day on which all men can be reunited in their primal oneness in God. Heschel defends the traditional observance of the Sabbath but recognizes the validity of the modern adaptations. He reaches out beyond the Jewish community and invites all Americans to share in the Sabbath heritage. Like Kaplan, Heschel recognizes the need to describe the Sabbath in terms that all Americans can understand. Unlike him he takes these terms to be ones of criticism rather than of affirmation of the general culture.

Kaplan proceeds from the assumption that ritual must be in keeping with man's ordinary sense of morality and that biblical injunctions concerning Sabbath observance often conflict with that morality.[126] He points to the authoritarian and inflexible attitudes they reflect and contrasts these with modern man's individualism and freedom. The only ritualism that has a chance of mobilizing man's spiritual powers today is one that respects independence and allows individuals the right to choose which observances to keep and which to reject. Could Kaplan sanction the total rejection of the Sabbath as a Jewish holiday? Hardly, because it is one of the foremost cultural productions of the Jewish people. While acceptance of the Sabbath in its authoritarian form is moral suicide, rejection of the Sabbath as a Jewish cultural treasure is ethnic self-destruction. Kaplan demands that Jews neither go to "the one extreme of rigid adherence to the minutiae of observance or to the other extreme of complete repudiation of the Sabbath as a whole. Jews will have to acquire that power of mental adjustment and spiritual plasticity which is essential in an age of transition like ours."[128]

If the criteria for the observance of Sabbath rituals are not the internal traditional ones, does the individual have a standard to guide him? Kaplan suggests that a ritual may be tested in terms of its power to enable man's utilization of his environment. Sabbath observances have meaning by their effect on man's conception of his context; ritual must be appropriate to that context. An individual can judge the value of the Sabbath from a study of "the affirmative conduct which the observance of the Sabbath will elicit from him."[129]

Kaplan self-consciously rejects the traditional myth of creation and claims that modern Jews are not motivated by the Genesis narrative in their Sabbath practice. "We observe the seventh day Sabbath," he comments, "not so much because of the account of its origin in Genesis, as because of the role it has come to play in the spiritual life of our People and of mankind."[130] The double nature of this comment can be made clear. On the one hand it negates the meticulous legalism associated with the creation myth. The Sabbath is no longer a recreation of a primal event and as such does not require exacting reduplication of divine activity. On the other hand the Sabbath is seen as an important element in man's spiritual existence. The Jew grows as a human being when he finds in observance of the Sabbath a religious lesson and spiritual nourishment. The function of the Sabbath is that of "making us truly human and helping us to transcend those instincts and passions that are part of our heritage from the sub-human."[131] We can recognize in this motivation a modern mythological affirmation: religious man helps humanize the modern world. Religious man spiritualizes the technological world in which we moderns live and as such makes it more fit for human life. "Human culture," Kaplan contends, "cannot dispense with symbolic forms for conveying spiritual values."[132] Modern man, according to Kaplan, is trapped in technology. He has forgotten art; he has become so involved in details that he has lost sight of the grander goal. The Sabbath is a means of recalling spiritual values and concentrating on the purpose and meaning of life. To survive as men we need the Sabbath:

> The present condition of western civilization, with its failure of nerve, may be traced to the sense of frustration which man now experiences . . . There is an urgent need for a renewal of that faith in life which Jewish religion proclaimed when it identified God with creation.[133]

Kaplan does not reject the biblical mythology. He reinterprets it. He is aware that modern man needs a new myth--a myth which we have seen him associate with religion. He finds the roots of that myth in the Jewish Sabbath, even though the myth itself conflicts with that which originally animated the ritual. Why, Kaplan demands, was the Sabbath instituted? If ritual is a code conveying values, what message lies behind the Sabbath? Kaplan seeks a naturalistic myth, a myth that will remind man not of a transcendent reality but of real opportunities for self-transcendence in everyday experience. His myth of the

Sabbath portrays it as an indication of just such opportunities. To call the world a creation of God suggests, for Kaplan, that the world possesses the tools man needs for his self-fulfillment; the Sabbath, on this account, "was designed to make the Jew aware that God provided him with the means and opportunities for the satisfaction of those desires that gave meaning and purpose to his life."[134] Kaplan utilizes the Sabbath as a ritual which draws attention to the abundance of man's environment. The Sabbath accomplishes this goal by symbolizing in religious terms what man experiences pragmatically in daily life. The Sabbath reminds the Jew of events in which he found his life supplied with meaning. It helps him recognize that "God is experienced as Creator, every time our thought of Him furnishes us an escape from the sense of frustration and supplies us with a feeling of permanence in the midst of universal flux."[135] The Sabbath offers a time of reflection during which a man can learn to designate certain aspects of his life as religiously relevant. What Sabbath ritual provides is a means of symbolizing the positive forces in life. The primary feeling of the Sabbath, for Kaplan, is one of gratitude. By using a modernized ritual and selecting personally relevant religious symbols Kaplan refashions the Sabbath into a statement of man's gratitude for his environment. Jews observing the Sabbath are transformed into model citizens, learning thankfulness, teaching a confused modern man to use ritual as a means of "evaluating the work of the week in the light of his highest personal and social ideals, profoundly grateful for what has been achieved and eagerly and hopefully expectant of future achievement."[136] We should note that Kaplan does not suggest what rituals should be retained or how they symbolize man's optimistic view of the world. He assumes that the community will evolve new rituals to convey the message that the traditional Sabbath once communicated.

Here we find Kaplan's basic approach illustrated. He reduces the meaning of a ritual to a set of theoretical ideas--Sabbath ritual expresses in ritual language a philosophical affirmation of man's experience. He does not explain why Americans need this ritual or how non-Jews can experience it. He is more concerned with showing the fit between the *ideas* animating the traditional Sabbath and those needed in American life. But in that concern he is also ignoring social reality. How can a thinker contend with the structural fact of religious pluralism? How is the Sabbath to transcend its parochial ritualism? These are unanswered questions. Even the ideals which the Sabbath represents are common not to humanity as humanity, but to democracy as a social form. It is impossible not to question Kaplan's assumptions that these ideals actually exist.

Abraham Heschel, on the other hand, is concerned with just these issues. He extends the meaning of the Sabbath from a concern for Jews to a significance for all humanity. In order to do this, however, he does more than point to the abstract message of ethics and idealism found in the Sabbath. He recognizes that many of the rituals associated with Sabbath observance are impossible not only for non-Jews but also for Jews. In order to accommodate this modern situation Heschel seeks for a way to avoid a dependency upon ritual. While Kaplan bases his ritualism on the contention that the Sabbath creates the religious atmosphere needed for ethical life, Heschel denies this. The Sabbath is rather a way of calling attention to a reality that already exists. Here the ecumenical perspective gives a hint about religious pluralism. There is a need for religious diversity, for ritual differences, because individuals respond to the same reality in different ways. Rituals can differ because they are all equally powerful guideposts pointing to an identical reality. The nature of that reality is also important. Unlike Kaplan, Heschel finds that reality beyond social life. The Sabbath symbolizes man's liberation from the everyday realities of competition and struggle. The Sabbath does more than project an optimistic view of reality; it supplies an alternative to it.

What is the Sabbath, Heschel asks. Utilizing a far more traditional language than Kaplan he answers that it is an intimation of eternity. Mankind, he suggests, lives in the realm of time. Man constantly fights against the elements; he seeks to change the empirical world so that it will produce more goods for him. Beyond the realm of time, however, is the sphere of eternity. Eternity, for Heschel, symbolizes perfect reality. It lies above all our efforts in time and by the perfection of its vision it directs them. The Sabbath does, it is true, consist of laws and obligations. Sabbath observance includes the ritual activities of lighting candles, refraining from work, changing one's behavior pattern. The Sabbath, it is also true, is signified by a special day, an hour in time. All that, however, is not essential. The essential power of the Sabbath lies in the glimpse it gives of a world beyond strife, of a period of peace and tranquility. For modern man the value of the Sabbath lies in this vision which can be achieved without the complicated ritualism. To participate in the Sabbath means, above everything else, to penetrate beyond the external reality of the world and to see its transcendent meaning. Heschel describes a traditional Sabbath, but this description points beyond itself to a transcendent significance for all mankind:

> An hour arrives like a guide and raises our minds above accustomed thought. People assemble to welcome the wonder of the seventh day, while the Sabbath sends out its presence over the fields, into our homes, into our hearts . . . Refreshed and renewed, attired in festive garments, with candles nodding dreamily to unutterable expectations, to intuitions of eternity, some of us are overcome with a feeling as if all they would say would be like a veil.[137]

Looking at this statement we can note several remarkable points. Unlike the traditional viewpoint, Heschel does not insist upon observance of meticulous details. While those details are present--festive attire, nodding candles--they are subordinate. Ritual accoutrements are reduced to associations with an independent metaphysical reality. The Sabbath comes into existence by itself, not even by "the hour," which appears merely as a guide. Heschel minimizes the importance of ritual activities. They are less important than an internal sense of a supreme reality. The Sabbath stands in its magnificence as a metaphysical homeland, the root of all existence and conveys the serenity associated with the "oceanic feeling" of returning home. Heschel in fact calls the Sabbath "our homeland, our source and destination," which provides us with "a profound conscious harmony of man and the world, a sympathy for all things and a participation in the spirit that unites what is below and what is above."[138] Confronted by this overwhelming reality, the significance of ritualism diminishes. The Sabbath is "an edifice in time"--a monument to eternity, and Heschel notes, "We often feel how poor the edifice would be were it built exclusively of our rituals and deeds which are so awkward and often so obtrusive."[139]

Because the Sabbath reunites man with his source it is an essential ingredient in our humanity. Heschel asks "is there any institution that holds out a greater hope for man's progress than the Sabbath?"[140] He supports his tacit implication that the Sabbath is indispensible by pointing to the ways in which it strengthens a sense of the unity of mankind, liberates man from trivialities, and prepares him for the challenges of modernity. The Sabbath solves "mankind's most vexing problems" by affirming "technical civilization, but in attaining some degree of independence from it."[141] Unlike Kaplan, Heschel does not see the Sabbath celebrating man's social environment. The Sabbath represents liberation from it: "It is a day of independence of social conditions."[142] Heschel argues for the necessity of such a perspective. Modern man has denied his inner reality. Concern with external demands for production, control, and manipulation have eroded man's responsiveness to his transcendent purpose. Man has, Heschel claims, become a slave to his environment; he constantly struggles to make his mark on the world outside. In so doing he has lost sight of the world within: "Nothing is as hard to suppress as the will to be a slave to one's own pettiness. Gallantly, ceaselessly, quietly, man must fight for inner liberty."[143]

Here is the mythological element corresponding to Kaplan's emphasis on the benign conditions of human existence. Heschel evokes a transcendent reality against which all the struggles and efforts of our divided lives pale. He challenges our technological concern for production with a vision of perfection and unified existence. In the light of this mythological realm of peace, tranquility, and spiritual living, everyday social battles lose their significance. A second element in Heschel's myth becomes evident when we focus on his restriction of the full experience to "some of us." Like Kaplan, Heschel too sees religious man as the prime mover in this mythology. Religious man conveys the tools by which a sensitivity to the Sabbath spirit is cultivated. Heschel's "religious man" while limited to "some of us" is not too exalted, not too extremely distant. Not only Kaplan, but Heschel as well recognizes the predicament of modernity. Heschel admits that "the ancient rabbis established a level of observance which is within the reach of exalted souls but not infrequently beyond the grasp of ordinary man."[144]

Heschel is sympathetic to modern man's desire to realize his latent religious potential. All men, he claims, can participate in religious man's experience no matter how minimal the amount of ritual practice performed might be. Sabbath ritual is indicative; it provides signposts pointing to religious experience. Each of the rituals involved "tries to direct the body and mind to the dimension of the holy."[145] Any one of the various Sabbath rituals can convey the basic message that all reality comes from one source and is an organic whole. Through any of the portals which Sabbath ritual opens a person can glimpse that holy center of life which endows all activity with meaning and significance. Prayer, Heschel suggests, "is not a need but an *ontological necessity*, an act that constitutes the very essence of man."[146] The Sabbath experience permits man to become human; it is an opportunity to perform that act which constitutes man as man. The significance of the Sabbath is extended beyond Jews to all humanity. All human beings who are responsive to the holy center of life share in the Sabbath experience. Not merely Jews but all religious men find their meaning affirmed in the dimension of the holy which the Sabbath ritual reveals. Because Heschel describes the Sabbath as "an island in time," as a reality which is waiting to be discovered, and relegates ritualism to the status of guideposts, he can expand the significance of the Sabbath beyond any parochial meaning. Sabbath experience need not be restricted to certain practices at certain hours performed by a certain religious group. It can be generalized as a human phenomenon, a generally human event of the spirit.

Like Kaplan, Heschel has focused on the myth of religious man as bearer of spiritual values and the Sabbath as indicative of those values. Like Kaplan he has justified a selective ritualism and substituted universalims for parochialism as the meaning of Sabbath observance. While differing in style and metaphysics the two theologians both accept the modern condition, the reduction of ritual performances, and the need to reinterpret the tradition. Both rearrange the Sabbath myth and ritual to evoke in modern man a response to the world in which he lives.

The difference between the two thinkers lies in part in their assessment of the meaning of modernity. For Kaplan it means a world-view in which supernaturalism is an outmoded conception, in which empirical fact is the only source of verification, and in which social life is the central reality. For Heschel modernity refers to a common religious predicament, an inaccessibility of man to the transcendent reality that lies in wait for him and without which his life lacks rooting in the divine. Kaplan confronts his perception of modernity with a transformed Judaism--a Judaism based on sociological studies, assumptions about human psychology and communal needs, a Judaism integrated with democratic ideology. Heschel, on the other hand, confronts his view of modernity with a transformed human being, a man sensitized through religion to his transcendent needs. Such a man, he holds, will be able to cope with the problems of modernity and despite the obstacles reattach himself to his transcendent source.

While certain attitudes that each thinker holds predispose them to one or another solution to modern man's problem we cannot underestimate the importance of their construction of the modern reality. It is because Heschel accepts the ecumenical perspective that he can speak so convincingly of the universal relevance of the Sabbath. It is because Kaplan does not share this view that the Sabbath becomes a cultural expression of certain universal ideals. While the distinction between transcendent and naturalistic religion is a basic one dividing Heschel and Kaplan, the ecumenical perspective also plays a role in separating them. Kaplan can advance the case for ritualism as a cultural expression. But this means that each culture group must have its own unique ritualism. Americans can give concrete form to their ideals by a set of American rituals, Jews by another. The two ritual systems can be reduced to the *same meaning* but one cannot substitute for the other. Heschel, however, finds in Judaism a recognition of a basic *religious fact*. The Sabbath is not a cultural creation but an ontological reality and because Heschel shares the ecumenical perspective he sees it as accessible to *all Americans*, beyond that to all who take the religious search seriously.

The Ecumenical Perspective and Jewish Ritual

On the question of ritual changes all four thinkers

agree that certain modifications are needed in the modern situation. Whether seen as a break with the past (Kaplan and Agus) or as an expression of ancient patterns (Heschel and Gordis) the reduction of practices and the reinterpretation of their meaning is enthusiastically accepted. All four thinkers struggle with the meaning of ritual and translate archaic symbols into the language of social unrest, personal dilemmas, or communal struggles. Yet Agus, Gordis, and Heschel have a particular outlook that separates them from Kaplan. Unlike him they seek to defend and legitimate more than the Jewish ritual tradition. Although they lavish their closest attention on Jewish prayer and Jewish religious practice, they include all religious forms in their discussions. They justify the religious endeavor *as such*.

The problem of defining a "civil religion" illustrates this difference between the two. Only Kaplan speaks explicitly of an American "civic religion." Yet it is clear that Heschel, Gordis, and Agus assume a basic religious commitment that permeates American society. Kaplan's "civic religion" develops out of his commitment to social pluralism. Since society is the basic reality, every social group must have its own ritualistic tradition. American Jews must, therefore, have two sets of rituals--one based upon Jewish social life and one evolved from American social experience. For those who share the ecumenical perspective each religious tradition is, by its very nature, an expression of the American civil commitment to religiousness. Its particular rituals are also the national rituals of American religious insight. No new rituals need to be invented. The biblical symbols--Sabbath, thanksgiving celebrations of whatever kind, worship wherever it takes place--are integrated into the fabric of Americanism through the established religious institutions. What is most important, according to them, is the establishing of a civil *attitude* which encourages each religious group and stimulate each individual to utilize those rituals accessible to him. While Kaplan finds that Judaism must be given a cultural sanction, the others demand that it be given a religious sanction. While Kaplan finds that all traditional rituals of all American culture groups must be refashioned in order to fit the alien message of modernity. The others see a variety of rituals each of which is intrinsically powerful in itself and can become a worthwhile part of modernity.

This difference between the ecumenical perspective and Kaplan can be traced to a divergent view of religious man's task. For Kaplan, it will be recalled, religious man draws a generalization about reality from empirical data. Ritual, then, is the symbolization of that generalization. American ritual and Jewish ritual can be reduced to the same function: they generalized about man's optimistic future in a supportive environment. Having made that claim it is natural for Kaplan to see the two rituals as overlapping. In fact one finds it hard to understand why there need be two of them at all. Religious man, it would appear, might fulfill his task of bringing good tidings to the world equally well as American or as Jew. Any person sensitive to reality should be able to generate a symbol of that optimistic future. Those who share the ecumenical perspective, however, are impelled to go beyond empirical data and everyday experience. They seek the depth-dimension of faith which transcends ordinary perception. Ritual becomes for them not a generalization about the world derived from experience but a key to transcendent knowledge which can be attained in no other way. Because the ecumenical perspective pays attention to what lies beyond empiricism the view of ritual espoused reflects a sense of transcendent reality. The ecumenical necessity to find a common ground beyond religious diversity is transformed in this theology of ritual. Ritual itself remains diverse just because it points to one reality--since men are tied to their social setting they can be liberated from it only by their own cultural tools. Kaplan justifies the continued practice of Jewish ritual on the basis of cultural pluralism--American social and civil life is enriched by the specifically Jewish culture represented. Heschel, Gordis and Agus legitimate particularistic rituals on the basis of a religious need arising from American social structure. Since American society is pluralistic and determined by historical and cultural diversity, the roads to self-transcendence can also be diverse. Beyond this these theologians offer Jewish ritualism to the community at large--it is a source of freedom not only for Jews but for all Americans.

The division between Kaplan and the other thinkers on the issues of civil ritual and the role of religious man reflect differing constructions of the world. Kaplan sees each culture as erecting its own social reality; American society and Jewish society certainly overlap but nonetheless retain their distinctiveness. The other thinkers take society no less seriously but do not draw distinctions between social groups. American society is understood as a complex interweaving of cultural subgroups; the same forces, however, impinge on all of them; they all face the same problems. Kaplan creates two ritual languages, one for each of the culture groups he envisions. The ecumenical theologians interpret the language of Jewish ritual as a disguised civil code. Kaplan locates the individual within society and sees in him a reflection of social life. The other thinkers discover the individual's reality beyond social life and find its significance in the way the individual emerges from private reality into public spheres. Kaplan demands a ritualism that identifies the individual's highest interests with those of society at large. Such a demand reflects his reluctance to posit the individual's reality as at variance with or even in distinction to social reality. Those sharing the ecumenical perspective are painfully aware of the two realities and the distance between them. They view ritual as an attempt to bridge the gap by transforming personal experience and thus influencing the social implications of that person's future action. Their analysis of ritual meaning and the ecumenical uses of a particularistic symbolism springs from their attempt to unite the personal world of religious oneness with the social experience of diversity and pluralism.

CHAPTER IV

EDUCATING FOR ECUMENICAL FAITH

While popular religious behavior had already decided the style of American Jewish ritual, Jewish thinkers had far more practical power in the structuring of Jewish education. The two components of the ecumenical perspective seem most in tension in this field. On the one hand Jewish education can be directed to survival, to group self-consciousness. The purpose of the curriculum and the schooling of children can be seen as that of maintaining Jewish identity. On the other hand Jewish education can take as its goal the cultivation of spiritual depths, the exploration of self, a discovery of meaning in the world. While the educational experience should at its best combine both technical competence and spiritual inspiration, in effect, pedagogues divide on just these issues. As with Jewish ritual so too with Jewish education there was considerable agreement about certain fundamental principles. Modernization as such was never questioned. The Jewish school was always thought of as part of American society and inculcating the basic ideals and values of that society. But the methods by which the Jew was taught to develop his potential, the basic ways in which Americanism and Judaism interrelated were conceived very differently by two schools of thought. These schools can be categorized chronologically. From the 1920s through the 1960s Mordecai Kaplan's influence was strongest; from the 1960s onward pedagogues illustrating what we have called the ecumenical perspective became more prominent. By the 1970s a new approach had developed which, however, lies outside the scope of this paper.

Two Types of Jewish Educational Philosophy

In 1969 a noted Jewish educator dramatically asked readers of a popular Jewish periodical "Are Our Religious Schools Obsolete?"[147] He focused his criticism on a pedagogy which stressed facts, skills, and information. In the place of these concerns he offered a program of values clarification in which the vitality of religious living is conveyed by a process of discovery rather than inculcation. The ideas he expressed were not really novel although they reached a wider and more popular audience through his article. Such an orientation to values and individualized learning, such a demand for flexible teaching techniques and alternative ways of communicating Judaism, was in fact a hallmark of the 1960s. The decade opened with Eugene B. Borowitz noting that in the 1950s "Jewish education was on the treshold of a new and more exalted status."[148] He recognized that the program of Jewish education initiated in the early 1900s and crystalized in the 1930s had achieved its acme in the fifties. Professionalized staffs, community schools, modernized textbooks and audio-visual aids, marked the success of this approach. Borowitz also pointed out, however, that the major task was that of discovering those values and ideals which are both "authentic to the Jewish past and integrated in the American present."[149] The new task of Jewish religious education would be to confront the spiritual crisis in American Judaism. At the end of the decade there could be no disputing of this new task. Eliezer Berkovits pointed to the decay of the public school system, once the strongest challenge to Jewish education, as a sign that "the competitor is no longer an authentic one."[150] Jewish education takes on new meaning, he suggested, when placed in the context of "the main features of the world-wide crisis that confronts mankind."[151] As the 1970s developed this approach became concretized in a number of alternative approaches to education--informal learning, camp programs, emphasis upon the affective realm of living became expressions of new pedagogical concerns.

The radical change initiated in the 1960s and made practical in the 1970s stands in sharp contrast to Jewish educational thinking during the earlier part of the century. The educational innovations introduced in 1910 by Samson Benderly and continued by his disciples throughout the United States represent a strikingly different view of the purpose of Jewish learning. This view stressed professionalization of teachers, community agencies and standards, and a curriculum which was "a conscious attempt to meld, if not impose, certain aspects of American life and thought with the raw material of the Jewish tradition."[152] As one of Benderley's leading students Emanuel Gamoran put it "The problem is one of transmitting the important values of the Jewish social heritage and at the same time of effecting an adequate adjustment to the conditions of American life."[153] Gamoran's influence dominated American Jewish education--and not merely the Reform Movement whose commission on education was indelibly stamped with his imprint. Efforts to restructure Jewish education focused on elevating its status, on bringing its organizational and pedagogical level up to that of the American public school system. A not inaccurate appraisal of this program of Jewish education called it a "Religious subsystem" which "culturally borrowed" its form and substance from the general environment.[154] Communal survival provided the basic impetus to Jewish education for these pedagogues while integration with the wider society provided the basic agenda.

This earlier form of Jewish pedagogical theory was self-consciously oriented towards American social life. The individualistic orientation of the newer style, however, can be deceptive. No less than their predecessors the thinkers of the 1960s were expressive of social tensions. In many ways they were conditioned by the same forces of the social structure. Their response can be seen as only an extremist version of the earlier theories. From a broader perspective both types of theologians served a common function; educators were participating in a basic social struggle, that between two contending parties of intellectual leaders. Hidden beneath the rhetoric of both types of Jewish pedagogical philosophies is a socio-political stance. Modernity includes both a widened sense of community and nationhood and an increasing atomization of tasks so that specialization of labor creates a heightened sense of alienation. Recognition of this basic contradiction in modernity is common to all Jewish educators and expresses the social reality that underlay their thought.

To demonstrate this contention we will look at Mordecai M. Kaplan, a foremost theologian and along with Benderly a molder of American Jewish education, in contrast to Abraham Joshua Heschel, one of the most articulate theologians of contemporary Jewish thought and from 1946 an educational leader in Conservative Judaism. Investigating these two thinkers we will find much that divides them. In temperament, style and theory they diverge drastically. Beyond this I think we will find that this divergence can be traced to the ecumenical perspective with the unity of function traceable to the social environment.

Restructuring Religious Education as a Social Subsystem

Mordecai M. Kaplan, who began his influential career as an exponent of modernizing Jewish education, argues that the relevance of Jewish learning depends upon its congruence with the American setting. Education has, or at least should have, as its overriding purpose the needs of the individual. The Jewish person requires an education that will afford him "maximum self-fulfillment as an American and as a Jew;" the task of the educator then is "to render the Jewish heritage relevant to his moral and spiritual needs."[155] Religious liberals should be entrusted with the task of developing such an educational system since traditionalists do not have the flexibility needed--in modern Jewish education Kaplan claims the task is "virtually to create the subject matter to be taught."[156] This subject matter should be that of the democratic way of life.

The study of Jewish subjects has as its purpose the training of "the young to regard all power which the individual possesses and acquires as misused, unless it is somehow shared with all mankind."[157] The entire Jewish tradition is pressed into service of universal goals and values. That within the Judaic heritage which exemplifies democratic ideals is to be stressed. History and literature should be subjected to a "modern interpretation" which "should focus on universal loyalty and responsibility as a means of developing ethical character."[158] While the curriculum of the Jewish school is particularistic--drawing on the national culture of the Jewish people--its ultimate purpose is universalistic: to create productive American citizens. Thus Kaplan claimed that democratic thinking, American values, and selfless devotion were "best conveyed through the Bible and the mass of Rabbinic lore based on it."[159]

Since the goal of Jewish education, according to this view, is the integration of Jewish and American studies it is not surprising that administrative and teaching techniques from the public school system were introduced by these educators into the Jewish classroom. The entire program of Jewish education was rennovated in order to bring the advances of modern schooling into Jewish learning. It would be a mistake, however, were one to regard the efforts and philosophy evolved as purely assimilationist.

Kaplan certainly did not see educational influence flowing in only one direction. Jewish studies could influence the public schools and inspire in them a greater religious sensitivity. Secular studies had "brought mankind to the edge of the abyss" and to save humanity religious values needed to be injected into schooling so that public schools could "train the student to share his powers with mankind."[160] Public schools were not expected to introduce Jewish subjects into their curriculum; that was unnecessary. The issue was not one of subject matter since the "subject matter taught in the public and high schools" is itself "a base for those human and spiritual values which would relate those studies to the task of building a better world."[161] If Judaism accepts the educational institutions of modernity, then modern schools should accept the educational aims and goals of American Jewry. The individual requires a coherent education in which there is a coordinated effort on the part of both secular and religious schools to inculcate American ideals. Public schools need not teach "theology," but they can teach American history in such a way that they reveal "God as manifest in American life."[162] Such a method of teaching secular subjects will reinforce the ways in which Jewish history is taught in the religious school. Institutional interaction can bring the techniques of the public schools into the Jewish classroom while introducing religious attitudes and values into the teaching of secular subjects in the public school system.

Kaplan's argumentation here assumes the existence of a religious element within American life itself. Secular education is being false to its own premises when it separates national concerns from religious concerns. American life is being torn apart by a false dichotomy:

> The spiritual dilemma in American life stems from the dichotomy between secular and spiritual education. That sharp division of educational functions has widened the gap between the secular and the spiritual interests of the American people.[163]

Kaplan viewed this division between the secular and the religious as a particularly dangerous one. His intuition that America's holidays, folklore, and general attitude towards life are the basis for a common sense of selfhood and identity (see above pp.   ff.) demanded an American consensus not only on matters of content but also on basic values. The public school could inculcate more than a generalized view of American history and an academic foundation for further study. Kaplan saw it as the breeding ground for American spirituality. While admitting that the public school has succeeded "in developing practical efficiency and patriotic sentiment," Kaplan also claimed that it should take as its goal "educating for decent human relations."[164]

How could a "secular" education develop means of attaining that latter goal? Kaplan's response to that question parallels his attitude towards Jewish educational modernization. Institutional innovation can enable the public schools to restructure their curriculum to emphasize humanistic values rather than merely preparation for economic success. The "religious" content of this curriculum would certainly be non-partisan; Kaplan saw it arising out of the American world experience rather than out of any particular religious tradition. Nevertheless textbooks, teachers, audio-visual aids could still be revised to make the depth-religious values of the American Way of Life more visable.

In his attitude towards both Jewish and public education Kaplan affirms the importance of structured, organizational techniques. His vision of an American system in which parochial religious schools inculcate national values and public education cultivates religious sensitivity was founded on a deep commitment to institutionalism. Textbooks, professionalized staffs, audio-visual aids, modernized techniques for presenting educational material, these were the clues to a fully unified program of learning. Kaplan saw in education a social system composed of a number of institutions working in harmony. The Jewish school itself was but a subsystem of the greater Jewish community which in turn was but a subculture of the total American civilization. As long as the institutions of the subsystem are prepared to follow the lead of those employed by the culture as a whole, there is no conflict. The child is socialized and educated in a single, consistent world-view and emerges from the process with a unified self-image. The essence of a democratic culture, as Kaplan analyzed it, lay in the responsiveness of the culture as a whole to its component subsystems. This responsive interplay of mutual influence was the basis of optimism and hopefulness on the part of these educators.

Religious Education as an Adversary to Institutionalism

Jewish educators since 1960 have not shared their predecessors' optimism. They demonstrate a marked aversion to institutionalism. While they stress universalism, democracy, and the integration of the individual they do not feel that structural changes of either Jewish or public schools will solve this problem. The earlier attempts failed, in their view, by assuming that education is transmitted from teacher to pupil. Learning, however, is a process. More must be asked of the child than that he memorize and repeat a set of facts or a list of ideas. He must become an active participant from whom creative thought is demanded. "The cardinal sin of our educational philosophy," Abraham Heschel told a While House Conference on Children and Youth, "is that we ask too little."[165] Kaplan's program, addressed to both public and religious schools, had assumed that teachers and a curriculum could solve spiritual problems. The dilemma of the separation between spiritual and secular life cannot be overcome through a parallel set of institutions. Only a transformed method of teaching can answer the modern need. The test of learning is not the ability to recall certain information but rather the "ability to ask the right questions."[166] Public schools inculcate rigidity and spiritual sterility by their concentration on facts alone; religious schools contribute to this error of focusing on history and customs without understanding their theological importance.[167] Merely teaching that Judaism has high values which are compatible with democracy is not enough. The Jew must learn to infuse social life with the spiritual insight of his tradition. Jewish education succeeds only "by cultivating empathy and reverence for others."[168] Such an education is directed to a person's self-image rather than his behavioral pattern. Rather than list the variety of Jewish observances and homiletically derive lessons for democracy from them, a true pedagogy of American Jewishness would delineate that task which faces the Jew in America.

Jewish education begins by demanding that the Jew regard himself in a new light. The goal of such education is the transformation of the Jew; what is required is that:

> every Jew become a representative of the Jewish spirit, that every Jew become aware that Judaism is the answer to ultimate problems of human existence and not merely a way of handling observances . . . Our goal must be to teach Judaism as a subject of ultimate personal significance.[169]

In the final statement we find the crucial difference between the two pedagogical views. Whereas the first approach seeks to present Judaism as an instrument of social change and development, the latter seeks to stress its relevance for the individual. The primary issue is "how young people can be brought up with a sense of responsibility in an affluent society."[170] The entire spectrum of Jewish studies--prayer, history, literature, philosophy--can be marshalled to evoke from the individual a response of spontaneous and willing participation in the democratic process. Religious education is entrusted with the task of molding the person, not of instructing a civil rights lawyer. Educational standards are to be adjusted so that learning ideas will become secondary to "an enhanced conception of man."[171] Study is not to be viewed as a means of acquiring certain skills, not as an instrument for self-centered professional advancement, but rather as "a form of worship, an act of inner purification."[172]

The practical program of education changes once these theoretical goals are accepted. Sensitivity to problems rather than mastery of a specific subject matter is crucial. Curriculum changes are less important than changes in teaching style. A student-centered education should be advocated in which the teacher is a facilitator of learning. The test of a teacher is not the amount of information conveyed but "the ability to let an idea happen."[173] Teaching, it is claimed, is "depersonalized;" impersonal and abstract ideas--democracy, freedom, liberty,--replace a living educational relationship between teacher and pupil. The teacher is not the autocrat of the classroom but "a midwife to the student."[174] It is possible to teach a "civilization;" instructors can convey those common elements between Judaism as an institutional system and American institutional life. But "civilization is our problem. Judaism is the art of surpassing civilization."[175] If the purpose of education is transforming the person then "it is not enough to impart *information*. We must strive to awaken *appreciation* as well."[176] Informal education, camp settings, creative classrooms, innovations in pedagogical technique were all part of the attempt to train the person rather than convey mere information.

Jewish Education and the Ecumenical Perspective

Can we trace the divergence between the earlier pedagogues and the later ones to the ecumenical perspective? In two basic ways the educational theory of the 1960s was based on the presumptions of that perspective. In the first place it rejected Kaplan's view of the interaction between public and religious schools. From the ecumenical perspective institutions are most productive when they are independent and challenge each other in their very self-sufficiency. Kaplan's thinking relies upon the interdependency of all America's school systems. He sees a creative exchange between secular and religious schools because each needs the others. The ecumenical perspective agrees on this mutual dependency but emphasizes that it is creative because each *challenges* the other rather than supports it. While for Kaplan the tension in modernity between administrative needs for experts and specialists and social needs for a communal identity and common system of values is *harmonized* in all facets of education, the ecumenical perspective denies the possibility of such harmonization. The relationship between administrative goals and humanistic ones is, for these latter thinkers, that of mutual tension; for Kaplan and the earlier thinkers it is one of interdependence.

Secondly because the ecumenical perspective focused

on values and the depth-dimension it could place the development of ideas rather than skills at the center of education. Despite Kaplan's advocacy of a spiritual component in all education he remained committed to the primary importance of teaching specialized skills--linguistic, cultural and academic--in both religious and secular schools. This emphasis gave special strength to his declaration that there is a need for both public and separate religious education. The skills needed by the American community are different than those needed by Jews. While integrated in their religious values the two school systems are separated by the skills they teach. For Heschel and the later thinkers, however, skills became secondary to the universal element which unites all mankind on the level of depth-religiousness. Institutional priorities become less important when the universal concerns of religious responsiveness replace the particularistic concerns manifest in the specific cultural skills of language and observance patterns.

Certainly the ecumenical perspective is not the entire, and perhaps not even the primary, element distinguishing Jewish pedagogy before and after 1960. Kaplan's view of religion as a cultural product led him to posit an almost inevitable American religion. Tutored by thinkers such as Will Herberg the later writers were--perhaps justly--suspicious of "the American Way of Life" and its claims to religious authenticity. Yet when we look at the way in which Jewish pedagogues sought to modernize Judaism the importance of the ecumenical perspective cannot be minimized. The essential question in modernization of religious education is that of its structural function. How does religious education play a social role in modern society? Both types of Jewish educators saw this role in terms of the struggle between administrators seeking specialists and experts who can carry out tasks quickly and efficiently and ideologues seeking to construct a cohesive social identity. The older view stressed the possibility of reconciliation and compromise; administrative and ideological goals can be brought together through institutional changes. The ecumenical perspective, however, is committed to the dualism of depth-religiousness in opposition to externalism, to universalism in contrast to particularism, to personalism in conflict with conformity. Accepting this dualistic world-view the ecumenical perspective could hardly help but perceive of religious man as an adversary to institutionalism. Pedagogues accepting this point of view fell very naturally into an adversary role in their educational philosophies. In this way the ecumenical perspective and the mythic world it represented sought to shape a generation of school children and to determine their educational experience.

CHAPTER V

THE SYMBOLISM OF ZION: A HUMANISTIC POLITICS

Zionism as Political Symbol: Beyond Liberalism

The common sense of modernity which binds Agus, Gordis, Heschel and Kaplan in their exposition of Jewish ritual is also present in their theology of politics. All four thinkers affirm the necessity for religion to be politically active; all four accept a humanistic universalism as the foundation for a religious involvement in civil life. Perhaps one can call the assurance with which they proclaim religion's task as a challenge to society a peculiarly American trait. Certainly the "prophetic" attitude of religion standing over and against the social order is not universally accepted across the globe. Nevertheless it seems to be a basic ingredient in American religious thinking. Protestant leaders, including both optimists like Walter Rauschenbusch and pessimists like Reinhold Niebuhr, have spoken out in this tradition. Catholic thinkers from John Courtney Murray to Michael Novak conceive of such a dynamic interrelationship between religion and politics. It is not surprising that Jewish theologians should present a similar picture. At the same time Jews have evolved a peculiar symbol of their own--that of Zion. Israel and Zionism have become metaphors in the Jewish community for the Judaic political tradition. We shall see that these four theologians differ in their approaches to civil involvement, but they agree in using the symbolism of Zion to express their views. Once again we shall discover beneath similarities of language and presentation a deep-seated difference based upon the acceptance or rejection of the ecumenical perspective.

Our concern will be to investigate the meaning of "Zionism" for these thinkers. How is it transformed into a general political symbol rather than a parochial nationalism? How is it made to function as part of the myth of modern religious man? Beyond this we will ask how its influence shaped the general political concerns of these thinkers. Can a typology of Jewish political theology be derived from both the Zionism and the general political approach of these writers. Before we can answer these questions we must dispose of one, overly simplistic, response that is often given. Jewish politics has frequently been labeled "liberal" and explained as the result of traditional Jewish values. Lawrence Fuchs in his studies on American Jewish political life set the pattern which has remained constant: Jews are predominantly liberal because of the religious values into which they have been socialized.[177] Werner Cohen's insistence that historical conditions be regarded as the decisive factor in Jewish politics did not stop him from saying that Jew and non-Jew are separated by "a separation which remains rooted in minds on both sides at as deep a level as religious feeling per se."[178] While studies in more recent times--particularly of the 1960 presidential campaign--challenge this view it still remains pervasive. While some arguments suggest that historical or sociological rather than religious factors explain Jewish liberalism, proponents of the basic connection between the Judaic system of beliefs and democratic government, liberal programs, and left-wing politics remain vocal and convincing.[179]

The factual question of Jewish liberalism and its relationship to Jewish religiousness needs a detailed study and more extensive statistical data than have been gathered so far. The glib response that Jewish theological politics should be liberal and universalistic because that reflects its inner meaning is a problematic one, even if in time it may be proven accurate. The factual question, however, is not our primary one. We are raising questions about perceptions, about a theological mythology, self-consciously developed by Jewish thinkers. The more appropriate question is: how did they view Judaism and liberalism. We find that in the 1960s Jewish theologians were reluctant to connect Judaism with any specific political program. For these theologians a religious approach to politics indicated an attitude, a way of viewing the political process but not a particular political system:

> I do not believe that Judaism commits us to any specific social, political or ideological system . . . My Judaism tolerates and even stimulates the most extensive experimentation with sundry economic programs . . . The precise application of the ethical demands of Judaism may be subject to differing interpretations.[180]

The predominant feeling was that searching to find in Judaism that political ideal which would be a blueprint for democracy was futile. Varied and often contradictory political systems, it was argued, are compatible with Jewish religiousness. When Richard J. Israel, for example, examined the options open to the politically concerned Jew he concluded that no positive program of social action can be found within the Jewish tradition. The Bible, in his view, is not relevant as a modern code; traditional Jewish law cannot cope with personalism and the unique elements of modernity; Eastern European Jewry is a stimulating source of idealism but not a solid base for modern life; even "expediency" and "Jewish self-interest" is a misleading criterion for political action. His final suggestion is that the tradition be used by the Jew as a fund of learning and a resource for attitudes but not as a code of behavior.[181]

Liberalism represents a political program, a specific set of proposals for civil actions. Jewish theologians did not avoid such proposals but made the attitude towards politics in general the more central issue. What is at stake in those attitudes? How are Jews expected to view civil life, government, international relations? Perhaps the most potent symbol around which Jews mustered political activity was that of the State of Israel, of Zionism. By examining how theologians explained and expanded this political image we can uncover the structure of Jewish political theology they espoused.

Zionism and the Judaic Tradition

The Jewish concern for Zion--for the land of Israel as a religious symbol, rather than as a political entity alone--has a continuous history from the Bible to the present day. Side by side with a realistic assessment of national life Jewish thinkers developed a theology of politics.[182] American Jews have, in recent times, not merely continued this tradition but magnified it until it constitutes the very content of American Jewish religion.[183] The problem of this transformation is captured in a story told by Joseph Blau. A Jew, it is told, changed from one synagogue to another because the rabbi of the first spoke more about the State of Israel than he did about God.[184] Such a Zionist focus is not uncommon; whereas traditionally the symbol of God provided the locus for Jewish hopes and ethical ideals with Zion as a tangential concern, in modern America the situation is reversed.

This reversal indicates that there is a myth being evolved. Certainly a realistic appraisal of the State of Israel--its goals, methods, and achievements--would reveal something less than an ideal standard of political behavior. Yet American Jews fail to see Zion realistically. It has become in their consciousness a symbol of political ideals, of lofty goals of international peace and brotherhood, a condensed symbol of prophetic insights. Zionism is viewed as the metaphor through which the true nature of Judaism is expressed, the symbolic representation of Jewish soul. The actual day to day life of Jews in Israel, the often less than ideal measures taken by the Iraeli government are beside the point. Zion stands for an idea rather than a reality. One may quarrel with this view. Certainly issues are confused when a modern state becomes transformed into a metaphysical symbol. It is not easy to sort out nationalistic pride and idealistic religiousness.

Political religion can be dangerously close to nationalistic idolatry. This study is not attempting to justify either the mythology of Zionism or its confusion of the ideal and the reality. It is, however, essential to recognize that theologians have the myth in mind and not the actual state of Israel when they write of Zion.

The mythology of Zionism, Jacob Agus argues, is a reflection of the eternal tension within the Jewish soul between nationalism and internationalism. In biblical times this tension was represented by the conflict between the kings and priests on the one hand and the prophets on the other. Since biblical times Jewish history has, Agus affirms, continually exhibited a tension between a "quasi-prophetic" universalism and a parochialism "opposing and contradicting it."[185] In modern times this tension is expressed through Zionism which displays both a narrow nationalism and an idealistic universalism. While admitting that "it is difficult for outside observers to realize that Jewish nationalism was not atavistic and narrow," Agus insists that Zionism was "motivated by high and universal ideals of service to mankind . . . (of) contributing to the spiritual regeneration of all men."[186] Both the outside observer and the insider who sees the idealism of Zionism see correctly. Zionism itself is an ambivalent phenomenon. By projecting Zionism as the modern symbol of the elements contending within the Jewish soul, Agus can accept both its parochialism and its internationalism. Zionism is a symbolic symptom of Jewish life; its tensions help us diagnose the condition of Jewish existence. Zionism is the cause neither of Jewish universalism nor of Jewish chauvanism. Agus sees it rather as the mode by which these two qualities are expressed. Zionism is an ambivalent good because it is an accurate reflection of the modern Jew and expresses rather than judges his inner life. Zionism is an instrument of Jewish self-assertion which can be both the assertion of idealism or of cultural particularism:

> While expression was thus afforded to the humanitarian activity within the Jewish community, scope was given as well to feelings of despair and cynicism, of resentment and militancy toward the non-Jewish world in the Diaspora and in Zion itself.[187]

Agus has chosen one way to root Zionism in Jewish history--it is the modern expression of an ongoing polarity within Judaism. Robert Gordis offers a similar view drawn from the dynamics of Jewish history. Instead of viewing Zionism as an expression of the "Jewish soul" he sees its ambivalence as historically conditioned. Jews have tended, he suggests, to develop either diaspora communities oriented towards integration in the world of the non-Jew or self-contained islands of nationalistic culture. Biblical precedent demonstrates such a tension between Ezra's national homeland in Israel and the Babylonian Jewish community which stressed universalism. This tension however, was a useful one and initiated a dialogue between two facets of Jewish life. Zionism is the latest example of this dialogue. Jews in Israel need, he claims, to listen to the Jews in the diaspora while diaspora Jews require the inspiration that comes out of Zion. Both communities are needed if Judaism is to be fully realized. Israeli culture, he suggests, will "emphasize the distinctly Jewish elements" in the Judaic tradition and scholars in the diaspora will "trace the historic interaction of the Jewish people and of its neighbors throughout history."[188] Not only Gordis but Mordecai Kaplan as well bases the authenticity of both the modern State of Israel and the continued existence of the diaspora on historical precedent. Jewish survival, they argue, has been achieved by diversification and cultivation of variety. The tension between a nationalistic homeland and an international peoplehood preserves this flexibility and multifaceted approach. A modern Zionism that affirms both the State of Israel and Jews living outside of that state merely continues the basic historical experience of Jewish life.

Abraham Heschel's view of Zionism stands in sharp

contrast to those of the other three thinkers. He does not see Zionism as a continuation of an earlier religious structure, an eternal pattern in the Jewish soul, or a basic historical paradigm. Zionism is purely a metaphorical symbol which, like all such metaphors, serves to arouse religious response. Zionism is linked to traditional Judaism not so much by what it is as by what it does. Heschel exalts Zionism when it reminds us that "we are not free to repudiate the Bible."[189] The basic lessons which Heschel derives from Zion reborn are those which he also finds in the Bible and in Hasidic literature--thus Jerusalem stands not as a substantial lesson of its own but as "*a witness,* an echo of eternity;" its memories convey "the immortality of words, the eternity of moments;" the events of June 1967 were "a reminder of the power of God's mysterious promise to Abraham and a testimony to the fact that the people kept its pledge;" it is not out of place when Heschel remarks in his study of the State of Israel that "Jewish tradition, too, is the homeland."[190]

Heschel uses Zionism as a modern means of evoking the entire system of Jewish law and lore associated with the Judaic tradition. In 1968 when Heschel was honored on his sixtieth birthday, Martin Luther King, Jr. spoke of his civil concerns, other speakers mentioned his theology and his studies on prayer and symbolism. He chose to speak on the meaning of the land of Israel. The discussion that followed touched upon Heschel's view of American politics, his opposition to the war in Viet Nam, his theological opinions, topics apparently only tangential to his talk. In effect they were intrinsically related to it because Zionism was for Heschel the focus around which all of Jewish tradition could be organized.[191] Zionism is legitimated as a modern Jewish political symbol because it can generate specific memories and associations. In itself Zionism may be an ambivalent symbol, a less than fully developed religious stance, but as a metaphor alluding to the Jewish past, Heschel finds it a powerful modern expression of Judaism.

Zion: A Metaphor for Universal Human Interaction

As a political myth Zionism has two facets--the first is a reconstruction of the human community and the second is a reconstruction of the human soul. In both cases the myth declares that only by being self-asserting can one learn to appreciate others. On the structural level Zionism symbolizes the contention that world community is possible only when individual cultures affirm their uniqueness. Productive relationships between nations, the myth suggests, occur when one culture confronts another as an equal, when each is attuned to what can be learned from the other. In biblical language Zionism may be called modern prophecy. Robert Gordis claims that all the prophets "exemplify both nationalism and internationalism" and demonstrate that "love of one's own people and loyalty to humanity represent two concentric circles."[192] The democratic element in Judaism, Mordecai Kaplan explains, "finds expression in its two main strands: prophetism and Torah."[193] The prophetic concern for both the Jewish nation and for an international structure of interrelationships between nations activates the modern political myth of Jewish thinkers. The "unique glory of Judaism," Jacob Agus argues, is the ability of the prophets "to rise above the cramping confines of narrow national loyalties to recognize the wrong-doings of their own people . . . to dream of a united world unmarred by tribal jealousies and wars."[194]

The key word is "dream." All four thinkers were unquestionably inspired by the biblical account of Israel's prophets, but each recognized the structural impossibility of imposing the biblical pattern on modern society. The political myth which Jewish thinkers sought to evolve was a specifically American one. It wrestled with the peculiar circumstances of American Jewish life. Abraham Heschel self-consciously directed his thinking towards American politics. When challenged about the relevance of his theology of Israel to his very radical political image, Heschel responded that:

> We Jews must continue to be aware that we are part of America and have a responsibility to and for America; to be sure we are involved with our whole soul. And the life of Israel is our life. We have to understand the situation and pursue a delicate and responsible course of action.[195]

Heschel has caught an important element in the mythology of Zionism in America. Zionism is not merely a Jewish national movement--it is an expression of Jewish ambivalence. Unlike biblical prophecy which was rooted in a single national loyalty--while to be sure opposing this nationalism to a transcendental loyalty to God--modern Jewish universalism is based upon a dual political allegiance. Zionism as a symbol of internationalism grows out of an effort to bring these two loyalties into harmony. Gordis, for example, claims that only by fostering such dual loyalties can meaningful dialogue develop between nations. The cultures of "the United States and of Israel," he states, "are being interpreted to one another, to the mutual enrichment of both communities."[196] Such enrichment is possible because, Gordis argues, the Jews are a unique type of political unit. Their nationalism is less loyalty to a political system than faithfulness to "a common cultural heritage," and Jews are "united the world over by no central political allegiance, military power or geographical contiguity."[197] The paradigm for religious and political interaction among nations is that of the Jewish people: international political loyalties combined with a distinctive sense of self derived from a geographical and political cultural center. The Jewish example of cultural attachment to one center combined with political attachment to another can be a model for world cooperation.

Mordecai Kaplan makes the same argument although his vision of the Jewish people and Zionism is more organizational and institutional than that of Gordis. He suggests an official charter by which "World Jewry will have to constitute an international people with the Jewish community in the State of Israel as its nucleus." This charter would contain provisions for humanitarian goals and their implementation in the world community.[198] Beyond the charter Kaplan sees the reality of a democratic, organic, pluralistic Jewish community. The fact of the diaspora, of the variations in Jewish observance, custom, thought, and tradition which characterize modern Jewry entail a new type of political form. Theocracy is no longer the religious ideal--instead Kaplan claims true religion points to democratic government. Jews have experienced living in two cultures, they have adapted themselves to a variety of political options. Zionism cannot afford to overlook this social fact; the existence of the State of Israel, he claims, is the best example of democracy at work. Three elements are involved in this claim. First the World Zionist Movement is interpreted as a democratically constituted instrument of the Jewish People as a whole. Kaplan points to its ability to reflect the needs and desires of so diverse a group of Jews that only a fringe of fanatics voluntarily refuse to collaborate with it.[199] The second element involved is the *Histadrut* or Worker's Federation. Kaplan suggests that "The purpose of protecting the trade union interests of its members" is only secondary to the primary purpose which is "to pave the way for a workers' community in Eretz Yisrael."[200] Kaplan sees the workers as representing their own concerns and forming their own destiny as members of the *Histadrut* and as such participating in the most primary form of democracy. Finally he points to the political system in Israel and--even in later writings does not change this view--claims that self-government by minority groups is a characteristic of Israel. Political self-determination is, for Kaplan, a reality of the new State which merits the attention of all lovers of democracy.[201] It is on the basis of these three elements that Kaplan finds the State of Israel in particular and Zionism in general a symbol of democratic internationalism. The World Zionism Movement is international in scope, it unites individuals of different political loyalties and is responsive to these differences. The *Histadrut* and the Israeli political system, according to Kaplan, are examples of a democracy which respects and cultivates minority groups. He does not claim that theological insight produced this result. His emphasis is upon the social forces and conditions "which led to the adoption of that aim," forces and conditions he sees as peculiar to the Jewish People."[202] American Judaism can be an example of a community within a community. Israeli society can be an example of pure democracy. Together these two communites, Kaplan believes, can provide the needed pattern for democratic social life. This social reality, he claims, "offers the Jewish People the unprecedented opportunity to be the vanguard of democracy."[203]

Kaplan's views stand out once again for their optimistic appraisal of modern life. Unlike both Gordis and Heschel he does not see Israel politics as a challenge to parochialism. He assumes that it is inevitable that its structure will initiate a new stage in human political life. He is less wary about the problems of dual loyalty because, unlike the other three thinkers, he has not taken seriously the problems of non-Jewish groups in America. There is a caution in the ways in which Heschel, Gordis and Agus speak about the exchange between America and Israel. They couch their language in terms of cultural values, personal identity, and double responsibility. Kaplan, on the other hand, is more explicitly political. He seeks to use precise political models, to build a very specific type of communal structure. The Jewish example is more than an illustration of the ways in which certain cultural values can interrelate--it is a political program.

The reluctance of Heschel, Gordis, and Agus to see in Zionism the type of concrete political program which Kaplan does may, I think, be traced to the view of reality each holds. While Kaplan makes social life and the institutions of society primary, and thus emphasizes the particularistic role of each national group, those sharing the ecumenical perspective look for the common human element that pervades all social organizations. Kaplan's espousal of Israel as a model political unit reflects his desire for autonomous Jewish social legislation--a desire influenced in no small measure by the example of Eastern European Jewish life. The model of religion in America, however, which animates Heschel, Gordis, and Agus posits a common human religiousness which expresses itself no matter what the particular political system may happen to be. The ecumenical perspective leads Agus to distinguish between the nationalistic elements in Zionism and its universalist ideals which can inspire all religious people. When Heschel holds up Israel's symbolic power to evoke sympathy and response from world Jewry as an example for all Americans he gives evidence of the ecumenical perspective which construes religion as personal rather than nationalistic. Gordis reflects the same supposition when he suggests how American life benefits from a cultural exchange with Israel. Unlike Kaplan these thinkers find the idea of Zion a more powerful religious influence than the reality of the political state. Their Zionism sees Zion as a religious symbol, a political metaphor, a cipher for existing civil conditions and a symptom of contemporary social life.

Both theologians seem to be evolving theories without a realistic appraisal of external forces. Agus admits the difficulty with which non-Jews can comprehend his Zionism, but he clings to it nevertheless. Kaplan's assumption that culture legitimates itself leads him into a naive expectation that the social organization of one specific cultural group can be transferred to other groups merely on the basis of its philosophical value. A greater sensitivity to other institutions--such as that cultivated by the ecumenical perspective--would have tempered his Zionism.

Zionism as a Lesson in Responsibility

While a central mythologem in the complex of meanings

that make up Zionism is sociological, the personalistic and mystical dimension also finds its place. Zion as model for international cooperation is augmented by the mythologem of Zion as symbol of human interdependency. The concern which Jews throughout the world have for the State of Israel can be interpreted as an example of brotherly love. Abraham Heschel characterizes the Jewish response to June 1967 as a specific instance of general human brotherhood. He finds "a cure of the soul in the concern on the part of the Jews everywhere for the people who live in the State of Israel."[204] He argues that such concern demonstrates a deep-seated human sympathy; it is more than a political alliance. Jews feel for the problems and difficulties of other people, Heschel concludes. Heschel finds this ability to identify with other individuals the primary result of Zionist symbolism. Zion as a potent myth evokes Jewish self-identification with the Jews in Israel. For Heschel the ideology of Zionism is less political than humanistic. Zion proclaims the importance of individuals, of a struggling group of people deserted by all allies, isolated from all help, yet bound by the cords of humanity to all others. The supreme lesson of this humanistic Zionism for Heschel is "To be concerned for the security and well-being of man everywhere is a concern that we must cultivate all the time, without qualification."[205]

In 1958 Heschel shared the platform with Mordecai M. Kaplan in a discussion of "Yisrael: Am, Eretz, Medinah--Ideological Evaluation of Israel and the Diaspora."[206] Heschel reiterated his concern for the individual and opposed this view of Zionism to Kaplan's. Before investigating that view, however, it is important to note the point made by an astute commentator. "It is needless to say," he said, "that both Kaplan and Heschel share considerable common ground in one area, and take up contrasting positions in another. Regretfully, it seems that what they agree upon appears more controversial to some religious circles in America than the conflicting viewpoints each expounds separately."[207] Both Heschel and Kaplan see Zion as a religious symbol; both view it as a universal myth capable of transforming not only Jewish life but modern life as well. Heschel, however, finds that its message is addressed to the individual in his solitary religious life while Kaplan proclaims its social message to society at large. For Heschel Israel's existence is a call to man; it is a lesson that "one must live as if the redemption of all men depended upon the devotion of one's own life."[208] Israel's meaning for the Jew, and for mankind, Heschel suggests "is not an ideology, a matter of choice, it is an existential engagement, a matter of destiny."[209]

Zion functions as a symbol recalling humanity to its religious obligations. Heschel's Zionism is individualistic because Zion itself is a metaphor addressed to persons in their existential situation. Heschel draws no line between "politics" and "religion." The inevitable consequence of "religion" in the life of the person is to inspire and generate "political" activity. The test of a religious person, the crucible in which religion is "proven" is that of commonplace actions. Heschel affirms that "it is not by the rate act of greatness that character is determined, but by everyday actions."[210] The danger of grandiose gestures and political theory lies in the ease with which practical issues are forgotten. The religious task is to bring politics into contact with human suffering; the individual must be reminded that his task is to consecrate the everyday, to transform commonplace reality. The "burning issue" according to religion, Heschel claimed,

> does not lie in organizing solemn demonstrations, but in how we manage the commonplace. The prophet's field of concern is not the mysteries of heaven . . . but the blights of society, the affairs of the market place.[211]

In his various writings Heschel sought to find the appropriate religious symbol to express this conviction. His analysis of the Jews of Eastern Europe continually stresses the importance of the common man, the task of redeeming the ordinary, the danger of loss of touch with reality. He recognized that Eastern European Hasidism had a touchstone with which to judge their lives. They possessed in Jewish mysticism a symbol potent enough to motivate commited action--man is the key to redemption. Through the symbolism of a cosmic battle between forces of good and evil the Jews "realized the wide range of their responsibility."[212] Turning to biblical precedent Heschel found in the prophets a model for his political approach. The prophet discovered that "*History is a nightmare*"--human beings evade their responsibility and fall into corruption--yet their purpose was "to bring about righteousness in history, justice in society, piety in the people."[213] As with the mysticism of the Jew in Eastern Europe, so with the prophet; morality is derived from a sense of God's concern and need of man. The basic statement of the prophet, Heschel suggests, is that "Justice is more than an idea or a norm. Justice is a divine concern."[214] Any religious person who cares about God cannot help but care about society. Heschel interprets prophetic politics as an extension of a divine command issued to every man--a command to bring history into agreement with God's ideals. "Righteousness," viewed from this perspective, "is not just a value; it is God's part of human life, *God's stake in human history*."[215] No individual is free from the requirement to refashion society. If social ills persist, all individuals are implicated. The prophets, Heschel reminds his readers, are concerned with "the moral state of people," not with this or that moral or immoral state; while "few are guilty" in creating an immoral society, "all are responsible" because they bear the burden of God's demand upon them.[216]

Zionism represents an even more potent symbol of religious man's obligation to work for a transformed society. "The life in the land of Israel today," Heschel proclaims, "is a rehearsal, a test, a challenge to all of us."[217] Like the symbolism of prophecy and mysticism, Zion as a religious myth arouses man to activity. Zion's meaning is the same as that of prophecy--God expects and demands from each individual a contribution to the redemption of mankind:

> The ultimate meaning of the State of Israel must be seen in terms of the vision of the prophets: the redemption of all men. The religious duty of the Jew is to participate in the process of continuous redemption, in seeing that justice prevails over power, that awareness of God penetrates human understanding.[218]

How does Heschel justify this interpretation of Zion? Practically he does so by pointing to the Jewish refusal to overspiritualize the concept. Not merely "Jerusalem in heaven," but "Jerusalem on earth" is required by Jewish tradition. What happens to the heavenly Jerusalem, he writes, "depends upon the destiny of Jerusalem on earth . . . It is not enough to be concerned for the life to come. Our immediate concern must be with justice and compassion in life here and now . . . "[219] The very concrete reality of the State and its needs forces the individual to pay attention to petty details, to the commonplace. Secondly, Zion evokes strong emotions; it banishes indifference. "I am afraid of detachments, of indifference, of disjunctions," Heschel admits; the very wall of Jerusalem radiates passion and ecstacy: "These stones have a heart, a heart for all men. The Wall has a soul that radiates a presence."[220] These two realities--the involvement in the commonplace and the reawakening of passion--evoke what Heschel sees as a cleansed consciousness. Self-interest, narrow perspectives, insensitivity, are all banished. Exposure to Zion "is a non-deliberate way of expanding compassion, of understanding the nonfinality of current history."[221] Heschel sees a three-fold task--man must be aware of his responsibility to help redeem the world, he must be involved with the petty details of the everyday, and his consciousness must be broadened to include all mankind. Zion is, of course, a Jewish symbol and Heschel agrees that "the burden is upon us Jews." He adds, "but we will not and must not do it alone."[222] The task which

Zion symbolizes is an enormous one. It is nothing less than a restructuring of reality, a building of a new world. Zion as religious symbol points beyond the State of Israel to the state of the world. Man's ultimate destiny and humanity's true vocation are revealed in Zion's crisis. "All of us," Heschel says addressing both Jew and non-Jew, "must learn how to create in this dreadful emptiness of our lives, how to be illumined by a hope despite disaster and dismay."[223] He finds that Zion as a symbol of rebirth can point to this hope beyond disaster, this ability to create despite despair.

Heschel's commitment to the ecumenical perspective has led him to evolve a depth-theology from Jewish experience. While Jewish history in general and Zionism in particular are uniquely related to the Judaic experience, that experience points beyond itself. The ecumenical perspective suggests that despite different religious institutions there is one universal faith. Heschel offers a corollary to this: despite different religious histories there is but one universal message of history: God's redemptive power. Zionism is interpreted in the light of this one universal message. It is possible to suspect Heschel's Zionism of ulterior motives. His advocacy of Zionism came late in his career. Earlier he had limited its significance to Jews alone; his historical summaries are often sketched hastily and rely on his previous writings. Not unreasonably one could suggest that Heschel has manipulated a popular response to the June 1967 Arab-Israeli war to advance a more persuasive exposition of his theology. If this is what he did, then we have made an important discovery. The ecumenical perspective not only shaped his thinking about Zion but was the controlling force behind his political philosophy.

In both Heschel and in Gordis and Agus the theological myth of religious man as Promethean bringer of light and Job-like sufferer looking to a reality beyond the empirical world is deepened by the myth of religion as a political force. The civil significance of religion, according to this myth, is that it uncovers the productive social consequences of internationalism and focuses attention on man's capacity for sympathy with others. Unlike Kaplan who takes the image of Zion literally and stresses the concrete social structures involved, the ecumenical perspective influences thinkers to see religion's task as that of providing political metaphors, not political programs. More than ever we are justified in calling the ecumenical perspective a myth. It generates those symbols by which men interpret the social world to themselves. The social consciousness is imaged politically by the view of Zion as a cultural center which enriches American life by its mere existence. The personalist consciousness is transformed into the political symbol of universal human empathy; Zion represents that ability of human beings to feel the sufferings of others as their own without which no political structure could stand. Both the intuition of social pluralism and metaphysical unity associated with the ecumenical perspective become potent political symbols through the Zionism of these thinkers.

CHAPTER VI

THE MYTHIC REALITY OF MODERN JUDAISM

The Ecumenical Perspective and the Problem of Consciousness

Our investigations have shown how the ecumneical perspective shaped the theology, ritualism, pedagogy, and politics of certain Jewish thinkers. In each case we saw that this influence directed theologians to think in terms of the individual and his inner world or of society and its institutional structures. Whether concerned with the question of God's nature and its relationship to the various biblical communities or the issue of rituals and their revitalization, Jewish thinkers framed their problems in terms of private piety or public organizations. This duality appears as a constant theme despite the variety of proposals offered by the writers we have studied. While Heschel, for example, seems to stress the metaphysical reality of transcendence and the key which religious man holds to that reality, he does not ignore structural forces. While Agus and Gordis often focus more directly on institutional religion, they join Heschel in his concern for the private reality disclosed by inner sight. The theological efforts we have analyzed all seem to be attempts to bring the Judaic tradition into agreement with one of these two polar realities.

While modern man holds no exclusive claim either to the pietistic consciousness of an inner reality or the social awareness of institutional power, the unique combination of these two world-views has become a distinguishing mark of modern times. Alternate ways of explaining the world are certainly available. Were Judaism to have been completely comfortable with these dual constructions of the world both the tensions and varieties of theological options which we have traced would not have been present. Unlike other thinkers--Mordecai Kaplan, for example, Agus,

Gordis, and Heschel do not reconstruct the raw material of Judaism. They are less concerned with changing structures and dogmas than with relating existing ones to a new way of viewing reality. The basic concern of their theologies is to align Judaism with either personalist or social consciousness. Modernizing Judaism--whether the subject is God, ritual, education, or politics--means placing Jewish tradition within the framework of the new view of the world.

How reality is perceived also influences how one reacts to it; is reality to be accepted as is or is it to be transformed? The ecumenical perspective confirms the social consciousness: our social life is shaped by powerful forces acting upon us and molding us without our control. Social facts are to be accepted; the social world is a fact to be confronted. The implications of this approach are conservative. These thinkers strive to support and maintain an open, pluralistic society. They evolve a theology of social differentiation. Unlike others--again Kaplan comes to mind--they do not impose another social system or an alternative ritual program on existing structures. Instead they offer a deeply resonant myth with which to reinforce the pluralism that is already present. The same approach holds true in their advocacy of an inner reality. None of these thinkers defines and describes the nature of the transcendent reality which religion opens to the individual. Depth-theology is universal because it is private and individualized. Rather than project a specific image of transcendent truth these thinkers stress the need for an environment, a context, in which the person himself can discover and glimpse that reality, according to his own abilities. The creative force of the ecumenical perspective lies in its ability to generate a myth which legitimates both exploration of the individual's private world and support for the public institutions that shape social life.

The Ecumenical Myth: The Many Mansions of Religion

The ecumenical perspective as we have noted again and again is based upon two simple claims: religious pluralism is a creative social force and depth theology is a universal, human experience. Behind these claims, however, lies a complex mythology which incorporates an interpretation of God, ritual, education, and politics. We have looked at the component elements, the building blocks, as it were, of that myth. Now we will examine the structure as a whole. Martin Buber provides a striking metaphor to illustrate his conception of interreligious communication. "Each religion," he remarks, "is a house of the human soul longing for God, a house with windows and without a door."[224] Buber holds that each religion is self-contained and that members in one house can call to those in other homes only through open windows--since each house lacks a door none can enter into the reality of his fellow. Windows opening out to the world present an opportunity for comparing ideas but experiences cannot be shared. While religious goals, values, and ideals can be communicated the life of a religion is restricted to its own adherents.

In contrast to this image the three thinkers we have studied see religion as a hallway with numerous doors each opening into the general world. Religion is a passageway leading into either the common reality of universal faith or the common marketplace in which a productive exchange of views is the basis of social creativity. Theology, ritual, religious education, and politics are all doors leading into a world experience which extends beyond the confines of any one religious tradition.

The ecumenical perspective transformed theology--considerations of God's being and nature--into a doorway providing entrance to both social life and personal faith. On the one hand theology was a clear challenge with which one religious tradition encountered another. As Agus and Gordis construe it no one can become involved in Jewish or Christian thought, taking seriously the alternative views of Scripture which each group presents. Theology, far from locking one within one framework, stimulates communication and leads to an appreciation of diversity and difference. From the standpoint of biblical theology only a varied and pluralistic religious reality can do justice both to the infinitude of God and the multiplicity within the human soul. Taking God seriously, this ecumenical theology suggests, means taking pluralism seriously and entering into the diverse reality which is human religiousness.

Heschel's concern for faith and depth-theology leads him to emphasize the universal influence of a vision of God. In every case, he argues, a glimpse of transcendence leads man to question his own life and that of society. Theological thinking impels man to explore a reality beyond empirical experience--both within himself and in the world at large. For Heschel thinking about God opens a door to that transcendent realm in which all mankind and all reality are unified. Once again far from entrapping a person in parochial self-concern theology opens vistas on a universal perspective. For Heschel theology unlocks the door to a divine perspective from which vantage place all divisions and separations disappear.

While this ecumenical myth of theology is striking, thinkers since the Enlightenment have pointed to the links between Judaism and Christianity. More unusual is the way in which Jewish ritual is made to serve an ecumenical purpose. Even Will Herberg whose early explorations of the American Way of Life give an indication of the ecumenical perspective drew the line at Jewish ritual observances. While actively supporting the universal message of the Jewish-Christian Faith, Herberg still declared that laws such as Kashrut (the dietary regulations) and the sabbath regulations were exclusively Judaic.[225] Yet Gordis and Agus suggested that Jewish rituals are an answer to the specific problems and modern life and Heschel, whose treatment of these rituals is extensive and detailed, finds them worthy symbols accessible to all modern Americans. The

Sabbath itself becomes for Heschel a metaphor which all people trapped in modernity can use.

Ritualism is not intrinsically a door to social interaction but Gordis, Agus, and Heschel agree that in practice it must become such a gateway. Ritual reveals the poverty of our social life, the insufficiency of our daily activities. Such revelations stimulate us to greater concern for others; pedagogically they teach the necessity to advance beyond self to social involvement. These thinkers do not deny the difficulty they have in revitalizing Jewish ritual to serve these purposes. The ancient language of rituals and symbols had become indecipherable. All three thinkers advanced their own views on reawakening the power of symbolic language. Yet all three agreed on the ecumenical spirit which would animate that language. The myth they created is consistent in that one detail: ritual propels its observer into the mainstream of human life. No matter how specific or parochial the ritual might seem its basic import is that of universalism. As a key unlocking man's entrance into the metaphysical experience of human comradeship or as a suggestive indication of the depth of social disease ritual enables the individual to escape from the limitations of nationalism and selfishness. Ritual is modern and modernizes the Jew just because it inducts him into his universal task. It is an experience of the religious vocation in the modern world--revealing the social structures which support pluralism and pointing to the inner world of unity and truth which cannot be glimpsed by focusing on empirical evidence alone.

Methods of modernization are as important as the instruments by which Judaism transmits its religious message. Theology and ritual are only two aspects of that message. Religious education is one of the most important means by which the modern Jew learns his spiritual vocation. Once again a modern myth is evolved: Jewish education sensitizes the Jew to the potential of each individual and his religious independence. Education opens the doorway into social participation by giving a person strength and confidence in his religious vision. Unlike others who seek to restructure society and educational facilities, the ecumenical theologians use education to inculcate a basic mythology. Skills and facts are acquired only as a means to another end. The final goal is that of actualizing the individual's potential to cope with modern society. To achieve that goal both pluralistic religious institutions and an intense concern with personal values and ideals was advocated. The division between Jewish educators before and after the 1960s lay in the distinctive myths each affirmed. The earlier pedagogues held that modernity was characterized by certain techniques and procedures. Once the Jewish school came to resemble the public school it would be modern. The later educators saw that only as an education vitalized the institutional identity of individuals and strengthened a sense of commonality with all religious souls could it justify its claim to modernity. Heschel and those who supported him directed their attention to this problem. Modernity meant coping with both the reality of social institutions and the inherent spiritual worth of the individual's private vision. By assimilating Jewish education and the ecumenical perspective a new myth was created--that of a modern man whose religious sensitivity cultivated a universal concern. The expectations of the new Jewish education were built upon this myth; without the ecumenical myth the relationship between self-exploration and depth-religious values could not have been established.

The political orientation of these thinkers, no less than their pedagogy is rooted in mythology. We may have become so accustomed to regard politics and religion as in dialogue that we forget how revolutionary such a view can be. Contending that politics, far from being a neutral zone within which religious differences are irrelevant, is motivated by religious concerns can be dangerous. Parochial interests, questions of dual loyalty, special pleading can all arise from the collapse of a distinction between spiritual and political goals. Such a merging of concerns, however, was imperative for the ecumenical myth. Political activism was projected as yet another door leading from Judaism to participation in modern society. The biblical record was construed so as to provide examples which might demonstrate that religious ideals must be translated into daily activities. More than this the specific Jewish concerns with Israel and Zionism were converted into symbols of modernity. The universalistic implications that Agus, Gordis, and Heschel draw from Zionism are truly striking. Zionism emerges as a metaphor for modern politics rather than as a Jewish political issue. The dangers and possibilities of religious pluralism are evoked by Zionism, according to the exposition of Agus and Gordis. Heschel interprets Israel's love of Zion as a spiritual force which is but one example of humanity's ability to emphathize with others who suffer. Zion becomes a modern religious ideal because it serves to illuminate both the structural reality of pluralism and the personal reality of religious vision. Zionism gains its power not from the practical politics which animates the various programs and organizations in American Jewish life, but it is claimed, from its compatibility with the basic orientation of modern man. The ecumenical perspective adds to Zionism the mythology of a depth commitment to human life and personal achievement, transforming a political platform into a religious mythology.

The common theme behind these expositions of theology, ritual, education and politics is that of entrance into the modern world. Behind the ecumenical perspective is the myth of religion as a portal into modernity. Energizing the efforts of Agus, Gordis, and Heschel is the conviction that religious man can move from one room of modernity to another, from one mansion to a second, by means of his particular tradition. Religion provides the keys to unlock the passage ways into the social world of politics, institutionalized organizations, and educational foundations. It also opens the doors leading to a private confrontation with ultimate reality. Religion illuminates the social arena so that the unified existence behind the diverse exterior becomes transparent. Modernizing Judaism means, according to this myth, discovering those keys Jewish religion provides so that individuals can open selected doors to universal experience and social living.

Modernization and the Development of Jewish Religion

Reading theology is dangerous and seductive. One is drawn into a universe of discourse that utilizes images and metaphors, freighted language and dense parables. Heschel's language, for example, abounds in a poetic use of evocative words; Agus employs philosophical categories in a creative and challenging way; Gordis conveys his ideas in a precise, scholarly fashion which belies the intensity of commitment which churns beneath the surface. It is astounding to recognize that this poetry, philosophy, and scholarship represents a grappling with the problems of modernity. One must be wary of accepting too readily the picture of modern life and modern consciousness that lies behind the ecumenical perspective. Certainly the temptation is present to claim that Agus, Gordis, and Heschel have indeed found the key to modernizing Judaism. Having decoded their very different theologies and found a basic agreement, excitement may lead us to a premature affirmation of their views.

This study does not suggest that Judaism is a modern religion or that the three theologians investigated represent the most modern approach to the Jewish tradition. What is striking is that three important and perceptive Jewish writers should have imperceptively constructed a compelling myth of modernity. What implications can be drawn from this finding? Here I think this examination produces some important results. Modernity is not merely a set of technological advancements. It is more than a syndrome of attitudes towards work, politics, education, and private life. Modernity can also be construed as a way of viewing reality; it may be what Wuthnow calls a "consciousness" or a combination of types of consciousness. Our investigation of Gordis, Agus, and Heschel has discovered that at least for them modernity meant such a perspective, and modernizing Judaism meant creating a Judaic mythology that could be consistent with that consciousness. Whether they were correct in their perceptions or not is less important than the mere fact that they created an entire mythology of Jewish theology, ritual, education, and politics based upon it.

Students of religion who investigate the phenomena of secularization, adaptation to modernity, and adjustment to new cultural contexts, will need to keep alert for changes in just this type of theological thinking. The macro-changes of ritual, dogma, political movements and educational structures are certainly indications of modernization. Yet more subtle developments are also possible. The construction of a new framework, a basic mythology that lies latent behind other changes and adaptations needs to be studied as well. How a culture creates an alternative mythology and what the basis for that mythology is requires investigation. The relationship between the ecumenical perspective, the social consciousness and the personalist consciousness, and the new Jewish mythology provides an instructive example. A modernized mythology may be constructed on the basis of a simple perception of reality. The ecumenical perspective demonstrates how two elemental convictions--affirmation of pluralism and of inner reality --can influence an entire complex of religious ideas. Shaped by this perspective theology, ritual, education and politics were transformed. Looking at each area individually the student would certainly be rewarded by insights into the modernization process. Without glimpsing the ecumenical perspective, however, the intimate connection between these areas might be ignored. This exercise in decoding the mythology behind three theological approaches to modern Judaism should be a useful model. Perhaps other Jewish thinkers and other religious groups with their own theological concerns will display a similar pattern.

Other studies along this line of inquiry would certainly be productive. This particular investigation of three thinkers is, however, helpful in itself. It draws attention to the way in which thoughtful Jews construed their predicament in America. As they wrestled with the demands of modernity and the problems of maintaining their own tradition these thinkers turned to myth-making. We should never forget that such creative production of myths is not limited to the distant past. Moderns have as deep a need for myths by which reality is explained as did ancients. There can be no clearer indication of this fact of human life than the effort of these thinkers to construct a modern Jewish myth. The ecumenical perspective flourished for a time and now seems to eclipse. As a potent myth, however, it deserves attention and remains a remarkable achievement of American Jewish thinkers.

NOTES

[1]Abraham Joshua Heschel, "The Eternal Light: A Conversation with Dr. Abraham Joshua Heschel," National Broadcasting Company, Inc., 1973. Mimeograph, p. 13.

[2]Jacob Bernard Agus, *Dialogue and Tradition: The Challenges of Contemporary Judeo-Christian Thought* (New York: Abelard Schuman, 1971) p. 89.

[3]Abraham Joshua Heschel, "From Mission to Dialogue," *Conservative Judaism* XXXI:3 (Spring 1967) p. 1.

[4]Robert Gordis, *Judaism in a Christian World* (New York: McGraw-Hill Company, 1966) p. xxvii.

[5]For a study of how civil cooperation led to theological dialogue see Naomi W. Cohen, *Not Free to Desist: The American Jewish Committee 1906-1966* (Philadelphia: The Jewish Publication Society of America, 1972) pp. 455-500.

[6]There is an extensive literature on "modernization" as a process inclusive of economic, social, political, and cultural change. Some of the more influential writings on the subject include David E. Apter, *The Politics of Modernization* (Chicago: University of Chicago Press, 1965); Samuel Noah Eisenstadt, *Modernization: Protest and Change* (Englewood Cliffs, New Jersey: Prentice-Hall, 1966); *idem.*, *Tradition, Change, and Modernity* (New York: John Wiley and Sons, 1973); Eva Etzioni-Hulevy and Amitai Etzioni, editors, *Social Change: Sources, Patterns and Consequences*, second edition (New York: Basic Books, 1973); Alex Inkeles and David Horton Smith, *Becoming Modern: Individual Change in Six Developing Countries* (Cambridge: Harvard University Press, 1974); Daniel Lerner, *The Passing of Traditional Society* (New York: The Free Press, 1958); Marion Levy, *Modernization and the Structure of Societies* Volumes I and II (Princeton, New Jersey: Princeton University Press, 1966); *idem.*, *Modernization: Latecomers and Survivors* (New York: Basic Books, 1972); a recent book that focuses on the modernization of consciousness is particularly helpful: Robert Wuthnow, *The Consciousness Reformation* (Berkley: University of California Press, 1976).

[7]Agus, *Dialogue and Tradition*, p. 429.

[8]Abraham Joshua Heschel, *The Insecurity of Freedom: Essays in Applied Religion* (New York: Farrar, Straus, and Giroux, 1966) p. 182.

[9]Agus, *Dialogue and Tradition*, p. 65.

[10]Abraham Joshua Heschel, *Man is Not Alone: A Philosophy of Religion* (New York: Harper and Row, 1951) p. 171.

[11]Agus, *Dialogue and Tradition*, p. 86.

[12]Heschel, *Insecurity*, p. 180.

[13]David E. Apter, "Political Religion in the New Nations," in *Old Societies and New States: The Quest for Modernity in Asia and Africa*, edited by Clifford Geertz (New York: Macmillan, 1963) p. 91.

[14]Joseph R. Gusfeld, "Tradition and Modernity: Misplaced Polarities in the Study of Social Change," in Etzioni-Halevy and Etzioni, *Social Change*, p. 340.

[15]Samuel H. Miller, *Religion in a Technical Age* (Cambridge: Harvard University Press, 1968) pp. 27-28.

[16]*ibid.*, p. 3.

[17]Levy, *Structure of Societies* II, p. 616.

[18]R. Pinder, "Religious Change in the Process of Secularization," *The Sociological Review*, N.S., 19:3 (August 1971) p. 348.

[19]Abraham H. Maslow, *Religions, Values, and Peak-Experiences* (Columbus, Ohio: Ohio State University Press, 1964) p. 34.

[20]Gordon W. Allport, *The Individual and His Religion: A Psychological Interpretation* (New York: Macmillan, 1950) p. 26.

[21]Abner Cohen, *Two Dimensional Man: An Essay on the Anthropology of Power and Symbolism in Complex Society* (Berkeley: University of California Press, 1974) p. 23.

[22]Hugh Dalziel Duncan, *Symbols in Society* (New York: Oxford University Press, 1968) p. 22.

[23]Wuthnow, *Consciousness Reformation*, p. 65.

[24]*ibid.*, pp. 138-172.

[25]Erich Fromm, *Psychoanalysis and Religion* (New Haven: Yale University Press, 1950) p. 37.

[26]Allport, *Individual and Religion*, p. 64.

[27]*ibid.*, p. 65.

[28]Robert N. Bellah, *Beyond Belief: Essays on Religion in a Post-Traditional World* (New York: Harper and Row, 1970) p. 199.

[29] Erich Neumann, *Depth Psychology and a New Ethic*, translated by Eugene Rolfe (New York: Harper and Row, 1969) p. 134.

[30] *ibid.*

[31] Fromm, *Psychoanalysis and Religion*, p. 37.

[32] Allport, *Individual and Religion*, p. 68.

[33] Robert Gordis, *The Root and the Branch: Judaism and the Free Society* (Chicago: University of Chicago Press, 1962) p. 185.

[34] *ibid.*, p. 91.

[34a] Will Herberg, *Protestant-Catholic-Jew: An Essay in American Religious Sociology*, a new edition, completely revised (Garden City, New York: Doubleday and Company, 1960).

[35] *ibid.*

[36] Robert Gordis, *A Faith for Moderns*, second edition (New York: Bloch Publishing Company, 1971) p. 49.

[37] Gordis, *Faith for Moderns*, pp. 75-76.

[38] *ibid.*, p. 295.

[39] Gordis, *Root and Branch*, p. 56.

[40] Gordis, *Christian World*, p. 157.

[41] *ibid.*

[42] Gordis, *Faith for Moderns*, p. 314.

[43] Agus, *Dialogue and Tradition*, p. 44.

[44] *ibid.*, p. ix.

[45] *ibid.*, p. 356.

[46] *ibid.*, p. 87.

[47] *ibid.*, p. 65.

[48] Heschel, *Man is Not Alone*, p. 112.

[49] *ibid.*

[50] *ibid.*, p. 109.

[51] *ibid.*

[52]Heschel, *Man is Not Alone,* pp. 120, 125.

[53]*ibid.,* p. 219.

[54]Abraham Joshua Heschel, *God in Search of Man: A Philosophy of Judaism* (New York: Harper and Row, 1955) p. 382.

[55]*ibid.,* p. 383.

[56]Heschel, *Man is Not Alone,* pp. 292-292, 271.

[57]Mordecai M. Kaplan, *The Meaning of God in Modern Jewish Religion* (New York: The Reconstructionist Press, 1937) pp. 25ff; Mordecai M. Kaplan, *Judaism Without Supernaturalism: The Only Alternative to Orthodoxy and Secularism* (New York: The Reconstructionist Press, 1958) pp. 109-120; Mordecai M. Kaplan, *The Greater Judaism in the Making* New York: The Reconstructionist Press, 1960) pp. 498ff; Mordecai M. Kaplan, *Questions Jews Ask: Reconstructionist Answers* (New York: The Reconstructionist Press, 1966) pp. 77-144; Mordecai M. Kaplan and Arthur A. Cohen, *If Not Now, When?: Toward a Reconstitution of the Jewish People* (New York: Schocken, 1973) pp. 37-38, 56-59, 96-98.

[58]See Eliezer Berkovits, *Major Themes in Modern Philosophies of Judaism* (New York: Ktav, 1974) pp. 149-191; Arthur A. Cohen, *The Natural and Supernatural Jew: An Historical and Theological Introduction* (New York: Pantheon Books, 1962) pp. 213-215; a rather different criticism is brought by Eugene B. Borowitz, *A New Jewish Theology in the Making* (Philadelphia: Westminster Press, 1968) pp. 114ff.

[59]Berkovits, *Major Themes,* p. 175.

[60]Kaplan, *Future,* p. 182.

[61]*ibid.,* p. 259.

[62]Kaplan, *Meaning of God,* p. 25.

[63]*ibid.,* p. 26.

[64]*ibid.*

[65]*ibid.,* p. 31.

[66]Kaplan, *Judaism Without Supernaturalism,* p. 110.

[67]Kaplan, *Greater Judaism,* p. 509; *If Not Now,* p. 119.

[68]Kaplan, *Greater Judaism,* p. 459.

[69]Kaplan, *Ethical Nationhood,* p. 54.

[70]Kaplan, *Meaning of God*, p. 326.

[71]Kaplan, *Judaism Without Supernaturalism*, p. 75.

[72]Maurice Friedman, *The Hidden Human Image* (New York: Dell Publishing Company, 1974).

[73]Marshall Sklare and Joseph Greenblum, *Jewish Identity on the Suburban Frontier*, Lakeville Studies I, (New York: Basic Books, 1967) pp. 57-59; Marshall Sklare, *America's Jews* (New York: Random House, 1971) pp. 110-117; *idem.*, *Conservative Judaism: An American Religious Movement*, new augmented edition (New York: Schocken Books, 1972).

[74]Sklare, *America's Jews*, p. 112.

[75]Charles Liebman, *The Ambivalent American Jew: Politics, Religion and Family in American Jewish Life* (Philadelphia: Jewish Publication Society, 1973) pp. 42-87.

[76]Sklare, *Conservative Judaism*, p. 269.

[77]Raymond Firth, *Symbols: Private and Public* (Ithaca, New York: Cornell University Press, 1973) p. 20.

[70]Mircea Eliade, *Myths and Symbols: Studies in Religious Symbolism*, translated by Philip Mairet (New York: Sheed and Ward, 1969) p. 12.

[79]Gilbert Cope, "Symbols: Old and New," *Theology Today* (January 1961) p. 500.

[80]Mary Douglas, *Natural Symbols: Explorations in Cosmology*, Pantheon Books, (New York: Random House, 1970) p. 2.

[81]*ibid.*, p. x.

[82]Shlomo Deshen and Moshe Shokeid, *The Predicament of Homecoming* (Ithaca, New York: Cornell University Press, 1974) p. 159.

[83]*ibid.*, pp. 173ff.

[84]*ibid.*, p. 209.

[85]*Proceedings of the Rabbinical Assembly of America*, Volume XVII (1953) pp. 151-215.

[86]Abraham Joshua Heschel, "The Spirit of Jewish Prayer," *Proceedings* Vol. XVII, p. 158.

[87]*ibid.*, p. 173.

[88]*ibid.*, p. 169.

[89]*ibid.*, p. 204.

[90]Eugene Kohn, "The Spirit of Jewish Prayer," *Proceedings of the Rabbinical Assembly of America*, Vol. XVII (1953) pp. 179-197.

[91]Heschel, *God in Search*, p. 357; Robert Gordis, *Judaism for the Modern Age* (New York: Farrar, Straus and Cudaly, 1955) pp. 187-189.

[92]Gordis, *Faith*, p. 291.

[93]Heschel, *God in Search*, pp. 287, 312, 316.

[94]*ibid.*, pp. 302, 303.

[95]Gordis, *Christian World*, p. 200.

[96]Heschel, *Insecurity*, p. 205.

[97]Gordis, *Modern Age*, pp. 189-190.

[98]Heschel, *God in Search*, pp. 356-357.

[99]Heschel, *Insecurity*, p. 192.

[100]*ibid.*, p. 18.

[101]Gordis, *Faith*, p. 291.

[102]Robert Gordis, "A Modern Approach to a Living Halacha," *Tradition and Change*, Mordecai Waxman, editor (New York: Burning Bush Press, 1958) p. 390.

[103]Robert Gordis, "Toward a Revitalization of Halakhah in Conservative Judaism," *Conservative Judaism* XXV:3 (1970) pp. 49-55.

[104]Abraham Joshua Heschel, *Man's Quest for God: Studies in Prayer and Symbolism* (New York: Charles Scribner's Sons, 1954) p. 112.

[105]Kaplan, *Judaism Without Supernaturalism*, p. 48.

[106]*ibid.*, p. 52.

[107]*ibid.*, p. 53.

[108]*ibid.*, p. 49.

[109]*ibid.*

[110]*ibid.*, p. 141.

[111]*ibid.*, p. 48.

[112]*ibid.*, p. 104.

[113] *ibid.*, p. 98.

[114] Kaplan, *Meaning of God*, pp. 124, 215, 270, 278, 284, 295.

[115] Kaplan, *Judaism Without Supernaturalism*, p. 102.

[116] Bellah, *Beyond Belief*, p. 168.

[117] Mordecai Kaplan, Eugene Koh, and J. Paul Williams, *The Faith of America* (New York: Reconstructionist Press, 1951) p. xxv.

[118] Agus, *Dialogue and Tradition*, pp. 529-531.

[119] Jacob B. Agus, *Guideposts in Modern Judaism: An Analysis of Current Trends in Jewish Thought* (New York: Bloch Publishing Company, 1954) p. 303.

[120] Sklare, *Jewish Identity*, p. 62; Leonard J. Fein, et. al., *Reform is a Verb: Notes on Reform and Reforming Jews*, (New York: Union of American Hebrew Congregations, 1972) p. 29.

[121] Fein, *Reform is a Verb*, p. 28.

[122] Sidney Goldstein and Calvin Goldscheider, *Jewish Americans: Three Generations in a Jewish Community* (Englewood Cliffs: Prentice-Hall, 1968) p. 229.

[123] Liebman, *Ambivalent American Jew*, p. 55.

[124] *ibid.*, pp. 40-41.

[125] Sklare, *Jewish Identity*, pp. 321-332.

[126] Kaplan, *Questions*, p. 109.

[127] *ibid.*, p. 115.

[128] Mordecai M. Kaplan, *Judaism as a Civilization* (New York: Macmillan, 1934) p. 447.

[129] *ibid.*, p. 445.

[130] Kaplan, *Judaism Without Supernaturalism*, p. 115.

[131] *ibid.*, p. 116.

[132] Kaplan, *Questions*, p. 227.

[133] Kaplan, *Meaning of God*, p. 69.

[134] *ibid.*, p. 42.

[135] *ibid.*, p. 78.

[136] *ibid.*, p. 81.

[137] Abraham Joshua Heschel, *The Sabbath: Its Meaning For Modern Man,* expanded edition (New York: Farrar, Straus and Company, 1963) pp. 66-67.

[138] *ibid.*, pp. 30, 31-32.

[139] *ibid.*, p. 15.

[140] *ibid.*, p. 40.

[141] *ibid.*, p. 28.

[142] *ibid.*, p. 30.

[143] *ibid.*, p. 89.

[144] *ibid.*, pp. 14-16.

[145] *ibid.*, p. 75.

[146] Heschel, *Man's Quest,* p. 78.

[147] Jack D. Spiro, "Are Our Religious Schools Obsolete?" *Dimensions* III:2 (1969) pp. 34-37.

[148] Eugene B. Borowitz, "Problems Facing Jewish Educational Philosophy in the Sixties," *American Jewish Year Book 1961,* Volume 62 (Philadelphia: Jewish Publication Society of America, 1961) p. 145.

[149] *ibid.*, p. 150.

[150] Eliezer Berkovits, "Jewish Education in a World Adrift," *Tradition* 11:3 (1970) p. 9.

[151] *ibid.*, p. 5.

[152] Walter I. Ackerman, "The Americanization of Jewish Education," *Judaism* 24:4 (1975) p. 419. Compare Oscar Janowsky, "Jewish Education" in *The American Jew: A Reappraisal,* edited by Oscar Janowsky (Philadelphia: Jewish Publication Society of America, 1965) pp. 123-172.

[153] Emanuel Gamoran, *Changing Conceptions of Jewish Education* (New York: Macmillan, 1925) p. 204.

[154] Norman L. Friedman, "Religion's Subsystem: Toward a Sociology of Jewish Education," *Sociology of Education* 42:1 (Winter 1969) pp. 104-113.

[155] Mordecai M. Kaplan, *The Future of the American Jew* (New York: Macmillan, 1948) p. 446.

[156] Mordecai M. Kaplan, *Judaism Without Supernaturalism*, p. 14.

[157] Kaplan, *Future*, p. 488.

[158] Kaplan, *Ethical Nationhood*, p. 69.

[159] Kaplan, *Future*, p. 187.

[160] *ibid.*, p. 488.

[161] *ibid.*, p. 489.

[162] *ibid.*, pp. 520-521.

[163] Kaplan, *Ethical Nationhood*, p. 156.

[164] Kaplan, *Questions*, p. 358.

[165] Heschel, *Insecurity*, p. 45.

[166] *ibid.*, p. 46.

[167] Abraham Joshua Heschel, "Teaching Jewish Theology in the Solomon Schechter Day School," *The Synagogue School*, XXVII:1 (Fall 1969), p. 16.

[168] Heschel, *Insecurity*, p. 159.

[169] *ibid.*, p. 234.

[170] *ibid.*, p. 44.

[171] *ibid.*, p. 50.

[172] *ibid.*, p. 57.

[173] *ibid.*

[174] *ibid.*, p. 55.

[175] *ibid.*, p. 233.

[176] *ibid.*, p. 236.

[177] Lawrence H. Fuchs, *The Political Behavior of American Jews* (Glencoe: Free Press, 1956).

[178] Werner Cohn, "The Politics of American Jews," in *The Jews: Social Patterns of an American Group*, edited by Marshall Sklare (New York: Free Press, 1958) p. 626.

[179] Compare the essays included in *Judaism and Human Rights*, edited by Milton R. Konvitz, B'nai B'rith Heritage Series, (New York: W. W. Horton and Company, 1972) with

Lucy Dawidowicz and Leon J. Goldstein, *Politics in a Pluralistic Democracy: Voting in the 1960 Election,* with a foreward by Richard M. Scammon (New York: Institute of Human Relations Press, 1963) pp. 94ff. and Edgar Litt, "Jewish Ethno-Religious Involvement and Political Liberalism," *Social Forces* 39 (May 1961) pp. 328-32; see also Liebman, *Ambivalent American Jew,* pp. 135-159.

[180]*The Condition of Jewish Belief,* compiled by the editors of *Commentary Magazine* (New York: Macmillan Company, 1966) pp. 130, 183, 227.

[181]Richard J. Israel, "Jewish Tradition and Political Action," in *Tradition and Contemporary Experience: Essays on Jewish Thought and Life,* edited by Alfred Jospe, a Hillel Book (New York: Schocken Books, 1970) pp. 189-204.

[182]Martin Buber, *On Zion: The History of an Idea,* with a new foreward by Nahum N. Glatzer (New York: Schocken Books, 1973).

[183]Liebman, *Ambivalent American Jew,* pp. 88-108; Joseph L. Blau, *Judaism in America: From Curiosity to Third Faith,* Chicago History of American Religion series, foreward by Martin E. Marty, series editor (Chicago: University of Chicago Press, 1976) pp. 73-90.

[184]Blau, *Judaism in America,* p. 205.

[185]Agus, *Dialogue and Tradition,* pp. 235, 423.

[186]*ibid.,* p. 192.

[187]Agus, *Guideposts,* p. 205.

[188]Gordis, *Christian World,* p. 205.

[189]Abraham Joshua Heschel, *Israel: An Echo of Eternity* (New York: Farrar, Straus and Giroux, 1969) pp. 45ff.

[190]*ibid.,* pp. 7, 15, 66, 211.

[191]Abraham Joshua Heschel, "The Theological Dimension of Medinat Yisrael," *Proceedings of the Rabbinical Assembly Sixty-Eighth Annual Convention,* 1968, Volume XXXII, pp. 91-113.

[192]Gordis, *Root and Branch,* p. 188.

[193]Kaplan, *Judaism Without Supernaturalism,* p. 77.

[194]Agus, *Guideposts,* p. 154.

[195]Heschel, "Theological Dimensions," p. 107.

[196]Gordis, *Christian World,* p. 121.

[197] Gordis, *Root and Branch*, p. 187.

[198] Mordecai M. Kaplan, *A New Zionism*, second enlarged edition (New York: Reconstructionist Press, 1959) p. 108.

[199] Kaplan, *Future of American Jew*, p. 364.

[200] *ibid.*, p. 369.

[201] *ibid.*, p. 370.

[202] *ibid.*, p. 371.

[203] Kaplan, *Judaism Without Supernaturalism*, p. 92.

[204] Heschel, *Echo*, p. 211.

[205] *ibid.*, pp. 220-221.

[206] Abraham Joshua Heschel and Mordecai M. Kaplan, "Yisrael: Am, Eretz, Medinah--Ideological Evaluation of Israel and Diaspora," *Proceedings of the Rabbinical Assembly Fifty-Eighth Convention, 1958*, Volume XXII, pp. 118-160.

[207] *ibid.*, p. 155.

[208] Heschel, *Echo*, p. 161.

[209] *ibid.*, p. 206.

[210] Heschel, *God in Search*, p. 384.

[211] Heschel, *Insecurity*, p. 43.

[212] Abraham Joshua Heschel, *The Earth Is the Lord's: The Inner Life of the Jew in Eastern Europe* (New York: Henry Schuman, 1950) p. 92.

[213] Abraham Joshua Heschel, *The Prophets* (New York: Harper and Row, Philadelphia: Jewish Publication Society of America, 1962) pp. 181, 361.

[214] *ibid.*, p. 32.

[215] *ibid.*, p. 198.

[216] *ibid.*, p. 16.

[217] Heschel, *Echo*, p. 224.

[218] *ibid.*, p. 225.

[219] *ibid.*, p. 147.

[220] *ibid.*, p. 20.

[221] *ibid.*, p. 23.

[222] *ibid.*, p. 222.

[223] *ibid.*

[224] Martin M. Buber, *A Believing Humanism: Gleanings*, translated and with an introduction by Maurice Friedman, Credo Perspectives (New York: Simon and Schuster, 1965) p. 115.

[225] Will Herberg, *Judaism and Modern Man: An Interpretation of Jewish Religion* (New York: Atheneum, 1970) p. 298.

BIBLIOGRAPHY

I. Jewish Theology

Agus, Jacob Bernard, *Guideposts in Modern Judaism: An Analysis of Current Trends in Jewish Thought.* New York: Bloch Publishing Company, 1954.

______, *Dialogue and Tradition: The Challenge of Contemporary Judeo-Christian Thought.* New York: Abelard Schuman, 1971.

Berkovits, Eliezer, *Major Themes in Modern Philosophies of Judaism.* New York: Ktav, 1974.

______, "Jewish Education in a World Adrift." *Tradition* 11:3 (1970) pp. 5-12.

Borowitz, Eugene B., *A New Jewish Theology in the Making.* Philadelphia: Westminster Press, 1968.

______, "Problems Facing Jewish Educational Philosophy in the Sixties," *American Jewish Year Book 1961,* volume 62. Phila-Jewish Publication Society of America, 1961, pp. 145-153.

Buber, Martin M., *A Believing Humanism: Gleanings,* translated and with an introduction by Maurice Friedman. Credo Perspectives. New York: Simon and Schuster, 1965.

______, *On Zion: The History of an Idea,* with a new foreward by Nahum N. Glatzer. New York: Schocken Books, 1973.

Cohen, Arthur A., *The Natural and Supernatural Jew: An Historical and Theological Introduction.* New York: Pantheon Books, 1962.

______, and Mordecai M. Kaplan, *If Not Now, When?: Toward a Reconstitution of the Jewish People.* New York: Schocken, 1973.

Commentary Magazine, editors, *The Condition of Jewish Belief: A Symposium.* Compiled by the Editors of Commentary Magazine. New York: Macmillan, 1966.

Friedman, Maurice, *The Hidden Human Image.* New York: Dell Publishing Company, 1974.

Gordis, Robert, *Judaism For the Modern Age.* New York: Farrar, Straus and Cudahy, 1955.

Gordis, Robert, *The Root and the Branch: Judaism and the Free Society*. Chicago: University of Chicago Press, 1962.

______, *Judaism in a Christian World*. New York: McGraw-Hill, 1966.

______, *A Faith For Moderns*, second edition. New York: Bloch Publishing, 1971.

______, "Toward a Revitalization of Halakhah in Conservative Judaism," *Conservative Judaism* XXV:3 (1970) pp. 49-55.

Herberg, Will, *Protestant-Catholic-Jew: An Essay* in American Religious Sociology, a new edition, completely revised. Garden City, New York: Doubleday and Company 1960.

______, *Judaism and Modern Man: An Interpretation of Jewish Religion*. New York: Atheneum, 1970.

Heschel, Abraham Joshua, *The Earth is the Lord's: The Inner Life of the Jew in Eastern Europe*. New York: Henry Schuman, 1950.

______, *Man is Not Alone: A Philosophy of Religion*. New York: Farrar, Straus and Young, Inc., 1951.

______, *Man's Quest for God: Studies in Prayer and Symbolism*. New York: Charles Scribner's Sons, 1954.

______, *God in Search of Man: A Philosophy of Judaism*. New York: Farrar, Straus and Cudahy, Inc., 1955.

______, *The Prophets*. New York: Harper and Row, Inc., 1962.

______, *The Sabbath: Its Meaning for Modern Man*, expanded edition. New York: Farrar, Straus and Company, 1963.

______, *The Insecurity of Freedom: Essays in Applied Religion*. New York: Farrar, Straus and Giroux, Inc., 1965.

______, *Who is Man?* Stanford, California: Stanford University Press, 1965.

______, *Israel: An Echo of Eternity*. New York: Farrar, Straus.

______, "From Mission to Dialogue," *Conservative Judaism* XXI:3 (Spring 1967) pp. 1-11.

______, "Teaching Jewish Theology in the Solomon Schechter Day School." *The Synagogue School* XXVIII:1 (Fall 1969) pp. 4-33.

Heschel, Abraham Joshua, "The Eternal Light: A Conversation with Dr. Abraham Joshua Heschel," National Broadcasting Company, Inc., 1973. Mimeographed.

Jospe, Alfred, editor, *Tradition and Contemporary Experience: Essays on Jewish Thought and Life.* A Hillel Book. New York: Schocken Books, 1970.

Kaplan, Mordecai M., *The Meaning of God in Modern Jewish Religion.* New York: The Reconstructionist Press, 1937.

______, *The Future of the American Jew.* New York: Macmillan, 1948.

______, *Judaism Without Supernaturalism: The Only Alternative to Orthodoxy and Secularism.* New York: The Reconstructionist Press, 1958.

______, *The Greater Judaism in the Making.* New York: The Reconstructionist Press, 1960.

______, *Questions Jews Ask: Reconstructionist Answers.* New York: The Reconstructionist Press, 1966.

______, *The Religion of Ethical Nationhood.* New York: Macmillan, 1970.

______, Eugene Kohn, and J. Paul Williams, *The Faith of America.* New York: The Reconstructionist Press, 1951.

Proceedings of the Rabbinical Assembly Fifty-Eighth Convention, 1958, Volume III, pp. 118-160.

Waxman, Mordecai, editor, *Tradition and Change.* New York: Burning Bush Press, 1958.

II. The Jewish Community

Ackerman, Walter I., "Jewish Education--For What?" *The American Jewish Year Book 1969,* Volume 70. Philadelphia: Jewish Publication Society of America, 1969, pp. 3-36.

Blau, Joseph L., *Judaism in America: From Curiosity to Third Faith.* Chicago History of American Religion Series, foreward by Martin Marty, series editor. Chicago: University of Chicago Press, 1976.

Cohen, Naomi W., *Not Free to Desist: The American Jewish Committee 1906-1966.* Philadelphia: The Jewish Publication Society of America, 1972.

Dawidowicz, Lucy and Leon J. Goldstein, *Politics in a Pluralistic Democracy: Voting in the 1960 Election,* with a foreward by Richard M. Scammon. New York: Institute of Human Relations Press, 1963.

Fein, Leonard, J., et. al., *Reform is a Verb: Notes on Reform and Reforming Jews.* New York: Union of American Hebrew Congregations, 1972.

Friedman, Norman L., "Religion's Subsystem: Toward a Sociology of Jewish Education." *Sociology of Education* 42:1 (Winter 1969) pp. 104-113.

Fuchs, Lawrence H., *The Political Behavior of American Jews.* Glencoe: Free Press, 1956.

Goldstein, Sidney and Calvin Goldscheider, *Jewish Americans: Three Generations in a Jewish Community.* Englewood Cliffs, New Jersey: Prentice Hall, 1968.

Janowsky, Oscar, editor, *The American Jew: A Reappraisal.* Philadelphia: Jewish Publication Society of America, 1965.

Konvitz, Milton R., editor, *Judaism and Human Rights,* B'nai B'rith Heritage Series. New York: W. W. Norton and Company, 1972.

Liebman, Charles, *The Ambivalent American Jew: Politics, Religion and Family in American Jewish Life.* Philadelphia: Jewish Publication Society of America, 1973.

Litt, Edgar, "Jewish Ethno-Religious Involvement and Political Liberalism." *Social Forces* 39 (May 1961) pp. 328-332.

Sklare, Marshall, *America's Jews.* New York: Random House, 1971

______, *Conservative Judaism: An American Religious Movement,* new augmented edition. New York: Schocken Books, 1972.

______, editor, *The Jews: Social Patterns of An American Group.* New York: Free Press, 1958.

______, and Joseph Greenblum, *Jewish Identity on the Suburban Frontier,* Lakeville Studies I. New York: Basic Books, 1967.

Spiro, Jack D., "Are Our Religious Schools Obsolete?" *Dimensions* III:2 (1969) pp. 34-37.

III. Studies of Modernization

Apter, David E., *The Politics of Modernization*. Chicago: University of Chicago Press, 1965.

_____, "Political Religion in the New Nations," *Old Societies and New States: The Quest for Modernity in Asia and Africa*, Clifford Geertz, editor. New York: Macmillan, 1963, pp. 57-101.

Eisenstadt, Samuel Noah, *Tradition, Change and Modernity*. New York: John Wiley and Sons, 1973.

Etzioni-Halevy, Eva and Amitai Etzioni, editors, *Social Change: Sources, Patterns and Consequences*. New York: Basic Books, 1973.

Geertz, Clifford, editor, *Old Societies and New States: The Quest for Modernity in Asia and Africa*. New York: Macmillan, 1963.

Inkeles, Alex and David Horton Smith, *Becoming Modern: Individual Change in Six Developing Countries*. Cambridge: Harvard University Press, 1974.

Levy, Marion, *Modernization and the Structure of Societies*, Volumes I and II. Princeton, New Jersey: Princeton University Press, 1966.

_____, *Modernization: Latecomers and Survivors*. New York: Basic Books, 1972.

Miller, Samuel H., *Religion in a Technical Age*. Cambridge: Harvard University Press, 1968.

Wuthnow, Robert, *The Consciousness Reformation*. Berkeley: University of California Press, 1976.

IV. General Sociology and Psychology of Religion

Allport, Gordon, *The Individual and His Religion: A Psychological Interpretation*. New York: Macmillan, 1950.

Bellah, Robert N., *Beyond Belief: Essays on Religion in a Post-Traditional World*. New York: Harper and Row, 1970.

Cohen, Abner, *Two-Dimensional Man: An Essay on the Anthropology of Power and Symbolism in Complex Society*. Berkeley: University of California Press, 1974.

Cope, Gilbert, "Symbols: Old and New," *Theology Today* XVII:4 (January 1961) pp. 498-500.

Douglas, Mary, *Natural Symbols: Explorations in Cosmology*, Pantheon Books. New York: Random House, 1970.

Duncan, Hugh Dalziel, *Symbols in Society*. New York: Oxford University Press, 1968.

Eliade, Mircea, *Myths and Symbols: Studies in Religious Symbolism*, translated by Philip Mairet. New York: Sheed and Ward, 1969.

Firth, Raymond, *Symbols Private and Public*, Ithaca, New York: Cornell University Press, 1973.

Fromm, Erich, *Psychoanalysis and Religion*. New Haven: Yale University Press, 1950.

Maslow, Abraham H., *Religions, Values and Peak-Experiences*. Columbus: Ohio State University Press, 1964.

Neumann, Erich, *Depth Psychology and a New Ethic*, translated by Eugene Rolfe. New York: Harper and Row, 1969.